## Charles Hodge

# Charles Hodge

S. Donald Fortson III

**EP** BOOKS

EP BOOKS
Faverdale North
Darlington
DL3 0PH, England

www.epbooks.org
sales@epbooks.org

EP BOOKS are distributed in the USA by:
JPL Fulfillment
3741 Linden Avenue Southeast,
Grand Rapids, MI 49548.

E-mail: sales@jplfulfillment.com
Tel: 877.683.6935

© Donald Fortson 2013. All rights reserved. No part of this publication may be reproduced, stored in a retrieval system or transmitted, in any form, or by any means, electronic, mechanical, photocopying, recording or otherwise, without the prior permission of the publishers.

First published 2013

British Library Cataloguing in Publication Data available
ISBN: 978-085234-927-4

*To*
*Tari Williamson and Jenni Pyrch*

## Contents

|  | Page |
|---|---|
| Timeline | 9 |
| Introduction | 11 |
| 1. Family and education | 13 |
| 2. The professor | 23 |
| 3. The great schism | 35 |
| 4. Seminary life | 51 |
| 5. The church question | 71 |
| 6. War and reunion | 91 |
| 7. Legacy | 105 |
| 8. The impact of Charles Hodge's life | 123 |
| Recommended reading | 127 |

# TIMELINE

1797  Birth in Philadelphia
1812  Princeton Seminary established
1814  Conversion at College of New Jersey
1819  Licensed by the Presbytery of Philadelphia
1821  Teacher of Biblical Languages at Princeton Seminary; ordination
1822  Professor of Oriental and Biblical Literature; marries Sarah Bache
1823  Birth of Archibald Alexander Hodge
1825  Founding of the *Biblical Repertory*
1826  Beginning of two-year study leave in Europe
1833  Struggle with lameness
1835  *Commentary on Romans* published
1837  Old School/New School schism
1840  Professor of Exegetical and Didactic Theology
1841  *Constitutional History of the Presbyterian Church in the U.S.; The Way of Life*
1845  Presbyterian General Assembly decides to rebaptize Roman Catholics

| | |
|---|---|
| 1848 | United States at war with Mexico |
| 1849 | Sarah Bache Hodge dies; 'Emancipation' |
| 1850 | Professor Samuel Miller dies |
| 1851 | Professor Archibald Alexander dies; *Uncle Tom's Cabin* |
| 1852 | Marries Mary Hunter Stockton |
| 1855 | 'What is Presbyterianism?' |
| 1857 | 'The Inspiration of Scripture' and 'Free Agency'; Dred Scott decision |
| 1858 | 'Adoption of the Confession of Faith'; New School Church schism |
| 1859 | John Brown's raid at Harper's Ferry |
| 1860 | General Assembly debate with James Henley Thornwell |
| 1861 | Civil War; 'The State of the Country'; Old School Church schism |
| 1864 | Old School/New School reunion in the South |
| 1865 | Abraham Lincoln assassinated; 'On Principles of Church Union' |
| 1867 | Presbyterian National Union Convention |
| 1869 | Old School/New School reunion in the North |
| 1870 | 'Retrospective of the History of the Princeton Review' |
| 1872 | Three-volume *Systematic Theology*; celebration of fifty years at Princeton |
| 1873 | Hugh Lenox Hodge dies; General Assembly visits Dr Hodge |
| 1874 | *What is Darwinism?* |
| 1876 | Benjamin Breckinridge Warfield graduates from Princeton |
| 1877 | Archibald Alexander Hodge joins Princeton faculty |
| 1878 | Charles Hodge dies at home |
| 1879 | *The Church and its Polity* |

# Introduction

In 1872 Professor Charles Hodge celebrated fifty years of teaching at Princeton Seminary in New Jersey. During this half century, Dr Hodge trained almost three thousand ministers, missionaries, and professors who had carried the gospel message throughout the United States and to many parts of the globe. During this period Princeton had been the premier seminary in the country, and no other teacher in America had come even close to instructing this many ministers during his career. Hodge not only shaped Presbyterianism and evangelical Christianity in his generation, but would have a lasting impact upon generations of clergy in America who devoured his writings and found in them a source of great intellectual and spiritual nourishment. On 24 April 1872, the seminary trustees honored Hodge with a public celebration at First Presbyterian Church in Princeton. Henry Boardman, one of the seminary trustees, addressed Hodge at the ceremony as 'a simple teacher of God's Word and defender of its truth'.

Four hundred of Hodge's former pupils were in attendance that day to honor their seventy-five-year-old professor.

To understand the power of Charles Hodge's immense influence on his myriad students and his widespread reputation as a Christian leader, one must consider his formative years as well as the mature theologian. It was his childhood experiences, his education, and the mentoring he received from other leaders, which shaped the young man who would become one of America's great nineteenth-century theologians. These relationships over a lifetime made him a man of substance who in turn had much to teach others. Hodge was a famous professor with a celebrated intellect; but what his friends and students admired most was his heart for God.

Hodge lived during an era of great crisis in the United States. Living for most of the nineteenth century, he would witness the abolition tumult of antebellum America, the bloody War Between the States, and the ongoing struggle of Reconstruction. His own Presbyterian Church would experience its greatest division during his lifetime. In the midst of these national and ecclesiastical calamities, the pen of Charles Hodge was active, constantly seeking to build bridges between adversaries. Though a peacemaker by demeanor, he understood that there was also a time to take a stand. And stand he did against the early waves of liberal theology that invaded America in the nineteenth century. Widely hailed as a defender of truth, Hodge battled a rising tide that was beginning to erode the sacred shorelines of historic Christianity.

# 1

# FAMILY AND EDUCATION

Charles Hodge's Presbyterian heritage ran deep and wide. His great-grandparents, William and Margaret Hodge, were Scots who had settled in Northern Ireland. Scots had been moving to Ireland ever since the reign of Queen Elizabeth in the sixteenth century. Many of these Scots-Irish practiced Presbyterianism, which they had brought with them from the homeland. William and Margaret Hodge had six children, three of whom immigrated to America in the 1730s after both parents had passed away. Three Hodge boys, William, Andrew, and Hugh, boarded a ship for the journey across the Atlantic and settled in Philadelphia. This was a period when hundreds of Scots were leaving Ireland and moving to the New World to settle in the colony of Pennsylvania.

The youngest of the three immigrant brothers, Hugh Hodge, became a deacon and founding member at Second Presbyterian Church in Philadelphia. The congregation was established in 1743 by a number of people converted under the preaching of George Whitefield who wished to organize a pro-revival Presbyterian church. Not all Presbyterians supported Whitefield, whose preaching would become a catalyst for the first major schism among American Presbyterians in the 1740s. One of Whitefield's strongest Presbyterian supporters, controversial revival preacher Gilbert Tennent, was the first pastor of Second Presbyterian.

Hugh's wife, Hannah Harkum, whom he married in 1745, was of French Huguenot descent on her mother's side. Hannah's family had been members of First Presbyterian Church in Philadelphia, whose pastor, Jedidiah Andrews, was one of the original seven clergymen who established the first American presbytery in 1706. First Presbyterian had been opposed to the 'enthusiasm' of Whitefield, but Hannah Hodge had been touched by Whitefield's ministry and joined Second Presbyterian. Hannah was known for her piety, hosting a weekly meeting for prayer and religious instruction in her home for many years after her husband died. She was Charles Hodge's great aunt, whom he remembered fondly from his childhood.

Another member of Philadelphia's Second Presbyterian was Hugh's older brother Andrew, who was Charles Hodge's grandfather. He was born in Ireland in 1711, coming to America in his twenties with his two brothers. In 1739, he married Jane M'Culloch, with whom he had fifteen children, although eight died in their infancy or at an early age. Andrew Hodge was a successful merchant in Philadelphia and owned a significant amount of property. A lifelong member of Second Presbyterian, Andrew Hodge served as a Trustee of the congregation until his death.

# Family and education

Charles Hodge's father, Hugh, was the eighth child born to Andrew and Jane Hodge, born in Philadelphia in 1755. Hugh Hodge attended the College of New Jersey (renamed Princeton University in 1897) and studied medicine, becoming a surgeon in the Continental army in the winter of 1776. Captured by the British, he was held prisoner in New York until his freedom was secured through the efforts of General Washington. After the War of Independence, he pursued business for a season and then returned to the practice of medicine. In the early 1790s there were several epidemics of yellow fever in the colonies and, while caring for patients, he was exposed to the disease. Hugh Hodge's own physical health was compromised, and he died at the age of forty-three in 1798.

The mother of Charles Hodge, Mary Blanchard Hodge, was a Bostonian, born in 1765. She was the youngest child of Joseph and Mary Blanchard, who both had died by the time she reached the age of twenty. Her parents being deceased, she moved to Philadelphia in 1785 to live with her brother John. In Philadelphia she was introduced to the Hodge family, marrying Hugh Hodge in 1790. Mary and Hugh Hodge lost their first three children to yellow fever or the measles when they were very small. However, a fourth child, Hugh Lenox Hodge, born in June 1796, would survive as Charles Hodge's only living sibling. Hugh Hodge Jr and his younger brother Charles would retain a close relationship throughout their lives.

Charles Hodge was born to Hugh and Mary Hodge in Philadelphia on 28 December 1797. Sadly, Charles would not know his father, for the senior Hodge died during the summer of 1798, just six months after his new son was born. Mary Hodge was left alone to raise her two boys, giving herself wholeheartedly to the task. Charles would write about his mother: 'To our mother, my brother and myself, under God, owe absolutely everything. To us she devoted her life. For us she prayed, labored and suffered.' Mary took responsibility for the spiritual nurture of the boys, taking them to worship on Sundays and drilling them on the questions and answers in the *Westminster Shorter Catechism*.

For a number of years, Mary and the two boys survived from the income from her father's docks and warehouse on Water Street Wharf in Philadelphia. When business on the wharf disappeared, she began to take in boarders to provide income for the family. Mary was a compassionate woman, helping provide necessities for the poor in her community. She was a founding member of a Philadelphia charity, the 'Female Association for the Relief of Widows and Single Women of Reduced Circumstances'.

The Hodge boys attended several schools for children taught by individuals in Philadelphia. Their lessons included reading, writing, arithmetic, and geography. They also received instruction at a drawing school, where Charles produced a watercolor landscape that would later hang in his study, eliciting admiration from friends and students. Hodge was amused at the notoriety given to this childhood painting, as he remembered his teacher looking over his shoulder and declaring, 'Charles, I think I could spit paint better than that.' In 1810, the brothers Hugh and Charles moved to Somerville, New Jersey, becoming boarders in several godly households while they studied Latin at a classical academy.

# Family and education

Mary moved with the boys to the village of Princeton in early 1812, renting a small house on Witherspoon Street, again taking in boarders to provide some family income. Hugh entered the College of New Jersey in May, while Charles, now fourteen years old, enrolled at Princeton Academy. This was a momentous move for young Charles Hodge, who would call Princeton home for the rest of his life.

The timing of the Hodge family's arrival at Princeton was noteworthy, for 1812 was the same year that the Presbyterian Seminary at Princeton would be established. The family already had personal connections to the new school through the president of its Board of Trustees, Ashbel Green. Ashbel Green had been the co-pastor of Second Presbyterian Church, performing the wedding ceremony for Mary and Hugh Hodge in Philadelphia. He had also assisted Mary in the religious education of her boys after Hugh Sr had passed away prematurely, tutoring the Hodge boys in the *Westminster Shorter Catechism*, which the boys memorized and recited to their pastor. Charles Hodge's life would intersect with Ashbel Green throughout his lifetime — early boyhood experiences, student days at the College of New Jersey and Princeton Seminary, and later as seminary professor.

As a young man, Ashbel Green had studied at the College of New Jersey under its famous Scottish president, John Witherspoon, the only clergyman to sign the Declaration of Independence. Witherspoon was notorious for his political views and keen intellect, but his primary legacy for many students was his understanding of Christian piety. Green had imbibed Witherspoon's philosophy concerning the centrality of religion to education. Witherspoon had stated, 'Learning without piety is pernicious to others, and ruinous to the possessor. Religion is the grand concern to us all, as we are men; — whatever our calling and profession, the salvation of our souls is the one thing needful.' Green embraced Witherspoon's perspective, and this was the educational philosophy that undergirded Hodge's schooling at both the College of New Jersey and Princeton Seminary.

In September 1812, Charles Hodge matriculated to the College of New Jersey, where Ashbel Green had just been appointed president. President Green encouraged revivals of religion on campus and stressed the importance of piety among the students, who attended Sunday afternoon Bible study and recited the *Catechism*. There was a revival on the campus in 1814 that touched a third of the student body. Seventeen-year-old Charles was among those who experienced an awakening and was converted. As a result, young Hodge made a public profession of faith in Christ and joined the Presbyterian Church in Princeton in January 1815. One of the preachers who spoke to the college students during the revival was Archibald Alexander, professor at the new seminary in Princeton which had opened just two years previously.

Archibald Alexander, a Virginian of Scots-Irish descent, had been converted as a teenager and licensed to preach by the age of nineteen. After initially serving two small congregations in Virginia, Alexander became president of Hampden-Sydney College, then pastor of the Pine Street Church in Philadelphia. In 1807, the Presbyterians selected Alexander as moderator of the General Assembly (national

# Family and education

body). Through his public advocacy of education for clergy, Alexander was instrumental in establishing Princeton Seminary in 1812. He was called to be the first professor of the new Presbyterian Seminary, where he would teach for four decades. Alexander encouraged godliness, daily meditation on Scripture, and the reading of Christian biographies among the seminary students. Fervent piety and moral character in ministers was equally important to sound doctrine at old Princeton Seminary. This emphasis came from Alexander, who was a role model for the young preachers.

Alexander would make a vast personal impact on the life of Charles Hodge. In later years, Hodge would write letters to his old mentor addressing him as 'my dear father'. As a teenager, Charles had attended the inauguration of Professor Alexander in August 1812. He had multiple encounters with him during his early years in Princeton village. Eventually, they would become colleagues on the Princeton Seminary faculty, and over the years of their relationship Alexander became a father figure to Hodge, taking him along on preaching tours and spending significant time in conversation. Their lives would be intertwined over many decades, and the imprint of Alexander's life upon Hodge was unmistakable. When Charles' first son was born, he named him Archibald Alexander Hodge (A. A. Hodge).

After finishing three years of study at the College of New Jersey, Charles Hodge entered Princeton Seminary in the fall of 1816. He was a diligent student and poured himself into his studies, which included work in Hebrew and Greek. In addition to his academic regimen, young Hodge attended the mid-week prayer meetings led by Dr Alexander, as well as the Sabbath afternoon conferences where professors and students would discuss 'experimental religion' (Christian living). These religious exercises made a deep impression on all the seminary students. Prayer, devotional reading of the Bible, and regular self-examination became a part of Hodge's life and shaped his conception of the ministry and the role of the seminary in inculcating serious Christian character among those studying for the ministry.

By 1819, twenty-two-year-old Charles Hodge had graduated from seminary and gone to live with his mother, who was back in Philadelphia. During this time in Philadelphia, he pursued further study of Hebrew under a tutor and attended lectures on anatomy and physiology at the University of Pennsylvania. In October of that year, in order to secure a license to preach, he was examined by the Presbytery of Philadelphia. Hodge had become a candidate for the ministry in 1817, presenting a Latin exegesis (theological paper) and preaching a sermon before the presbytery. The second step of licensure included examination in theology and church history, and giving a lecture on a portion of Scripture. These portions of the exam being sustained, Hodge was licensed along with a black man, Samuel Cornish, on 20 October 1819.

After his licensure, Hodge was assigned responsibilities to preach on Sundays at various missions in the Philadelphia area. Meanwhile, Archibald Alexander had discussed with Hodge the possibility of teaching Greek and Hebrew at Princeton Seminary, as the professors were looking for an assistant in this area. The funds were secured and young

# Family and education

Hodge was appointed by the professors to teach the original languages of Scripture for the annual salary of four hundred dollars. Hodge moved back to Princeton in June 1820 to begin preparations for his new role as instructor at the seminary. The Presbyterian General Assembly officially approved the seminary's employment of Hodge in May 1821 for a one-year term.

By this time Hodge had already transferred to the Presbytery of New Brunswick, which first appointed him as stated supply minister at Georgetown for six months, and then moved him to serve temporarily Trenton First Church in the fall. Teaching at the seminary and now with pastoral work as a licentiate, Hodge requested that his presbytery fully ordain him to the gospel ministry. For his ordination trials, he preached an assigned sermon on 1 Corinthians 1:21 and gave his testimony to 'experimental acquaintance with religion'. He was also examined in theology, natural and moral philosophy, church government, and the sacraments. Having successfully completed these examinations, Hodge was officially ordained on 28 November 1821 by the Presbytery of New Brunswick at Trenton First Church, along with two other ministers, the Rev. Dr Samuel Miller of Princeton Seminary presiding.

Hodge enthusiastically pursued his teaching career with a sense of God's providence in his life. His involvement with the lives of seminary students touched his life in powerful ways. One moving encounter was the sudden death of a student in February 1822. Writing to his mother about the experience of witnessing this young man's death, he recounted how the two professors (Alexander and Miller), along with other students, surrounded the dying man's bed, singing a hymn upon his request. He was impressed by the student's firm trust in Christ for salvation. Hodge wrote: 'I was also much impressed with the conviction of the truth and of the essential importance of some of the leading doctrines of the Bible, particularly that we are saved by faith, and only for the sake of what Christ had done and suffered for us.'

During this time, Alexander began to discuss with Hodge the possibility of his having a full-time position in the near future. However, there was concern that Hodge's name was not well known throughout the General Assembly, which would have to approve any appointment to permanent professorship. One of Alexander's ideas was to publish and circulate among the Presbyterian clergy a paper that Hodge had presented to students on biblical criticism. The new instructor, feeling the inadequacy of the paper, was not very keen on the idea, but acquiesced to the wishes of his older colleague. The paper was published as 'A Dissertation on the Importance of Biblical Literature'. Hodge was enjoying seminary teaching, and in a letter to Alexander he confessed his own sense of contentment at the seminary, but wanted to be sure this was God's will if he was to be a permanent faculty member. He wrote, 'With regard to the Professorship itself, I think now as I have always thought that it is decidedly the most eligible situation for improvement, for satisfaction and for usefulness, which our church affords.'

# 2

# THE PROFESSOR

Hodge was busy in his public life as a teacher at the seminary; but not too busy to carry on a courtship with a woman he dearly loved. On 19 June 1822, Charles Hodge married Sarah Bache, whom he had known since the two were teenagers. Her father, Dr William Bache of Philadelphia, a grandson of Benjamin Franklin, had passed away; so Mrs Catherine Bache and the children had moved into the Hodge home as boarders in 1813. Sarah, the oldest child in her family, was fourteen when the Bache and Hodge families began living together in Princeton. She soon won the affections of Charles, who was smitten by the young woman with dark auburn hair and big blue-gray eyes.

Charles and Sarah built a strong friendship, and one gets a glimpse of the spiritual quality of their relationship in the letters he wrote to her. Hodge was sensitive to the centrality of Christ in their relationship. In one letter to Sarah from his seminary student days, he bemoans how lately some of their letter-writing had dealt with trivial matters rather than spiritual things. In the letter he encouraged Sarah to 'look unto Jesus', reminding her that believers were to throw all upon Christ and trust his promise to deliver from sin. In another letter from seminary in 1818, he rehearsed some of the insights he had gleaned from Archibald Alexander in class, writing, 'There is more to be learned by prayer than by study.'

Sarah and Charles were finally able to marry in the summer of 1822 in a ceremony at Cheltenham, near Philadelphia. The officiating minister was Episcopalian Bishop William White, who had married Sarah's parents in 1797. The newly-wed couple lived in several Princeton dwellings before moving to the home they built on the seminary grounds across from Nassau Hall. This was the home where Charles would have his renowned study that welcomed his friends, colleagues and students during the many years of his professorship at the seminary.

In July 1823, the Hodges were blessed with their first son, whom they named Archibald Alexander. Two years later Mary Elizabeth was born. The Hodges would have six additional children during the 1830s, two more daughters and four sons. As a father, Charles made his children's spiritual lives a priority. A. A. Hodge recalled that his father always allowed the children free access to him in his home study, and this was later extended to the grandchildren. The senior Hodge led morning worship for the whole family, praying for the children and having them recite with him the *Apostles' Creed*. On the occasion of his daughter's baptism in December 1825, he wrote to his mother:

> *Your dear little Mary Elizabeth was baptized this afternoon in the Oratory by Dr Alexander ... I never appreciated so highly before the privilege of thus giving to God what is dearest to us on earth ... To be instrumental in thus training up one of the children of the Lord to be presented before Him without spot or blemish, is so delightful and honorable a task, that we cannot help hoping that He who has made the prospect of the duty so pleasant, will aid us in the performance ... Our dear little children we have promised to educate for heaven, and as God shall enable us, we mean to perform our vows. To this everything must be made secondary.*

After completing two successful years as a novice teacher, Hodge was appointed Professor of Oriental and Biblical Literature in May 1822 for an annual stipend of $1,000. When he was inaugurated as professor in September, the first words of his address were: 'The moral qualifications of an Interpreter of Scripture may all be included in Piety: which embraces humility, candor, and those views and feelings which can only result from the inward operation of the Holy Spirit.' This inaugural lecture set the tone for his entire ministry as a seminary professor who approached the sacred Scriptures with a humble spirit before almighty God, upon whom he would lean for illumination of the Word of God.

One of his principal early professorial labors was the founding in 1825 of the *Biblical Repertory*, one of the oldest quarterly journals in the United States. This nationally-recognized religious publication would consume considerable amounts of his time over the years. In its pages Hodge would address a broad range of subjects, which included not only theological topics and ecclesiastical issues but also politics, philosophy, culture, history, and science. While the scope of the *Biblical Repertory* would expand through the decades, its original purpose was to be a source for reprints of recently translated literature on Scripture coming out of Europe.

Hodge was increasingly sensitive to his own perceived inadequate knowledge of European learning, and decided that it would strengthen his own scholarship if he could study abroad. He was especially interested in studying further biblical languages and textual study in France and Germany. He broached the idea with the trustees, who concurred with his request and made provision for the new professor to take two years off from seminary duties in order to study with Europe's best scholars. This would be a life-changing experience for Hodge, who met many of Europe's prominent Bible scholars and theologians during his study leave abroad.

Planning for the overseas study involved making arrangements for Sarah Hodge and the children to live in Philadelphia with his mother. John W. Nevin, a recent Princeton graduate, would teach Hodge's courses at the seminary while he was in Europe. With provision for his family and teaching responsibilities arranged, Hodge departed in the fall of 1826 for the month-long voyage from New York to France. Arriving in Paris, he began language study, which included French, Arabic, and Syriac. After Paris, Hodge's journeys took him to Germany to study at the University of Halle, which had been the academic center of German pietism since the late seventeenth century. Pietism was a reactionary movement to the dead orthodoxy of the state Lutheran Church. It emphasized heart religion, holy living, and missions.

At Halle, Hodge studied with the renowned Hebrew scholar Wilhelm Gesenius, who personally tutored him for a semester. He employed a German tutor named George Müller, who would become legendary in later life for his faith-based orphanage in England. His most significant encounter at Halle was with theology professor August Tholuck, with whom he would build a friendship that lasted for the rest of his life. Tholuck was two years younger than Hodge, but impressed him with his learning and personal piety. Influenced by pietist teaching himself, Tholuck had embraced their ideals and opposed the rationalism that was rampant among German scholars. Writing decades later, Hodge admitted that the time spent with Tholuck was the most useful of all of his time spent in Europe.

In Berlin, the young Princeton professor met the remarkable church historian Johann August Wilhelm Neander, a converted Jew, author of numerous books on the Church Fathers and a six-volume *General Church History*. He also made the acquaintance of Ernst Wilhelm Hengstenberg, professor of oriental languages in Berlin, whose scholarship included many commentaries on books of the Bible. Hengstenberg was a traditional Lutheran and attacked the revisionist theology of other German thinkers like Friedrich Daniel Ernst Schleiermacher, who had made religious intuition and feeling the central element of Christianity rather than the historic Protestant principle of *sola scriptura*. Schleiermacher, sometimes called by historians the 'father of modern theology', was immensely influential on the following generation of theologians through his systematic theology, *The Christian Faith*.

Hodge kept a journal during the whirlwind two years abroad as a young man in his late twenties. Recording some of his impressions about both personalities and places, Hodge took full advantage of every occasion to learn new things. Experiencing Lutheran worship, he observed the formality of the Lord's Supper, which to him seemed very similar to Roman Catholicism. At a Reformed church in Halle, he observed the rite of Confirmation and was much impressed with the solemnity of the event and the opportunity it afforded young people to be recognized as church members. Though he had questions about the biblical warrant for this practice, he wondered whether a similar service introduced into Presbyterian churches could have a 'good effect'. While attending this service, he heard a hymn accompanied by the organ and four trumpets, recording in his journal, 'This is the first time I have heard this kind of music in a church. The effect upon my feelings was very strong and very pleasing.'

Hodge had the opportunity to hear the celebrated Schleiermacher preach some of his stirring sermons at his Berlin church. While Hodge rejected Schleiermacher's theological paradigm, he was, however, influenced by his friend Tholuck's appreciation for the good he could see in Schleiermacher's life and preaching. As a mature theologian Hodge would criticize Schleiermacher's view of the Bible, but acknowledged that he was a fellow Christian. This charitable spirit towards those with whom he strongly disagreed theologically would epitomize Hodge for the duration of his scholarly career.

In 1828, after saying farewell to his new Christian friends in Germany, Hodge began the long journey back to Princeton. On his trek home he travelled through France and Switzerland, viewing the Alps, whose beauty overwhelmed him. Going through England, he visited Cambridge and heard the elderly Anglican clergyman, Charles Simeon, preach. For fifty-four years, Simeon preached at Holy Trinity Church, ministering to multitudes of students over the years, about one thousand becoming ministers. Hodge also visited the Oxford colleges, and then traveled to Liverpool, where he boarded a ship in early August for the six-week voyage back to New York.

In mid-September 1828, thirty-year-old Charles Hodge arrived back in Princeton to a joyful reunion with his family. He resumed his teaching at the seminary, which now boasted over one hundred students. Hodge was asked to give the 'introductory lecture' at the seminary in November, which afforded him the opportunity to reflect publicly on what he had learned during his study abroad. His time in Europe had given him a deeper appreciation for the American church's freedom from state interference; yet one thing that had impressed him about public education in Prussia was the requirement for religious instruction. German boys and girls were taught essential Christian doctrine and morals as part of their regular school curriculum. Hodge stated in his lecture: 'The German system provides for education of Protestants, Catholics and Jews alike, and where it is possible, by separate schools. Is it not possible in this country to have the Christian religion taught in the common schools?'

One of the chief insights of his European experience was a fresh appreciation of the connection between piety and truth. After the sixteenth-century Protestant Reformation, the German church entered a period of 'cold orthodoxy' where the focus was upon intramural Protestant debate over fine points of doctrine. The seventeenth-century Pietist movement had been only a temporary reprieve to the diminishing spiritual life of the Germans. Here was the lesson for the American church: '... holiness is essential to correct knowledge of divine things, and the great security from error. And as you see, that when men lose the life of religion, they can believe the most monstrous doctrines, and glory in them; and that when the clergy once fall into such errors, generations perish before the slow course of reviving piety brings back the truth.' The vain speculations of the German theologians were a result of forsaking the Word of God and seeking truth in their own understanding. The inseparable link between personal piety and pure doctrine was confirmed for Hodge by his observations of what had evolved in European Christianity. He was determined that this would not be the case at Princeton Seminary.

Hodge picked up his teaching responsibilities again as Professor of Oriental and Biblical Literature. His teaching load included courses in Hebrew and Greek, survey courses on the Old and New Testaments, and exegesis classes on particular books of the Bible. Teaching Pauline Epistles directly from the Greek text in his hand, Hodge was especially adroit at gleaning central doctrinal points in biblical passages and focusing students' attention there rather than upon the technical points of critical exegetical questions. Students recalled that he would interject practical application into lectures, pointing them to the love of God for lost sinners. The contents of his biblical lectures were edited for publication as commentaries over the years.

His first published commentary was on the book of Romans in 1835. In consultation with Dr Alexander, Hodge decided to forego inclusion of Greek in the text in order to make it accessible to the English reader. Hodge accentuated the doctrinal contents of St Paul's epistle as he proceeded through the chapters of Romans, concluding each section with his practical remarks. This commentary was significant given the contemporary theological controversies swirling around Pauline teaching on the imputation of Adam's sin to all humanity (i.e. the doctrine of original sin). Several pastors and theologians of the era had published commentaries on Romans and Hodge added his as a defense of traditional Reformed theology based upon the explicit teaching of Scripture. Alexander was pleased with Hodge's first commentary, which would 'confirm the orthodox faith of our church'. The work received positive reviews immediately and was printed in an abridged edition for Bible classes in 1836. The commentary was popular in England and was translated into French by 1841.

During the initial years of his return to Princeton, Hodge was struck with a physical impairment in his right thigh which would incapacitate the professor for the rest of his life. He had had difficulty with the leg prior to his trip to Europe, but had not been troubled with it during his two years overseas. Upon his homecoming he was occasionally bothered with soreness in the leg, but by the summer months of 1833 it had become severe. In the spring of 1833, thirty-six-year-old Hodge had been tasked with raising funds for a new seminary chapel and had spent long hours walking through large sections of New York City canvassing Presbyterian churches. This had aggravated his condition to such a degree that by summer he was bed-ridden. With his leg in a splint, he stayed horizontal for a number of months until he became comfortable with sitting and standing again. All manner of treatments for his hip, thigh, and knee were attempted for the next few years, and gradually his leg was restored, though he would walk with a cane for the rest of his life. Walking remained difficult for Hodge, who wrote a note in June 1843 indicating that he had walked into Princeton village that day for the first time in ten years.

Because of the lameness, his study at home became a central gathering place for family, students, colleagues, and friends. Between the summer of 1833 and the winter of 1836, he held classes in his house, either in the back parlor of his home or in the study. There were two doors leading to the study; one on the outside for students to use and an internal door used by his children, who were always free to visit their father at any time. In this home study he would do his reading and writing over the next forty years. Seminary faculty meetings were held in Hodge's study, as well as meetings of the *Biblical Repertory* editors to discuss and review articles to be included in the journal.

While Hodge had been in Germany, Professor Robert B. Patton had served as the editor of the *Biblical Repertory*.

In 1829, the editorial oversight of the journal changed, as did its name, now *The Biblical Repertory and Theological Review*. An 'Association of Gentlemen in Princeton', one of whom was thirty-two-year-old Hodge, were to be the editors, reviewing all materials published in the journal. By 1837, the title was changed again to *The Biblical Repertory and Princeton Review*, a title it would carry until 1872, when it merged with another journal. Hodge would be the primary working editor of the *Review* until 1868, when Dr Lyman Atwater of Princeton College joined him as co-editor and took over the bulk of editorial labors.

A central piece of furniture in Hodge's study was a couch given to him by his brother Hugh. Hodge performed most of his labor as a professor lying upon this couch, especially in the years where his infirmity was most intense. Hugh was a Philadelphia doctor who became a professor in the medical department of the University of Pennsylvania. On several occasions the elder Hodge supplied his younger brother's needs, supplementing his income when the seminary was unable to pay Charles' salary. Less than two years apart, the brothers maintained a close relationship throughout their adult lives, keeping a steady correspondence between them. For a number of years, Charles wrote to his brother weekly, pouring out his heart upon the issues of the day and seeking his brother's counsel.

# 3

# THE GREAT SCHISM

An 1829 advertisement for the *Biblical Repertory* stated, 'The work is not designed to be controversial in its character, but to state temperately and mildly, yet firmly and fearlessly, Bible truth in its whole extent.' Hodge would become the major voice of this journal from the 1830s. Between January 1829 and April 1840, Hodge wrote thirty-six articles published in the *Biblical Repertory*. This was also the period when he received the Doctor of Divinity degree from Rutgers College in New Brunswick, New Jersey, thus becoming known to the seminary and the church as 'Dr Charles Hodge'.

In the 1830s, Dr Hodge's writing projects for the journal were often concerned with engaging the increasing discord within the Presbyterian Church. By this time two primary factions were present among Presbyterians, a traditionalist Old School party and a more innovative New School party. The differences were both theological and practical. On the doctrinal side, the Old School was concerned about the dilution of historic Calvinism among Presbyterian clergy. Some of the conflict was focused on an influential Congregational theologian named Nathaniel Taylor, who trained a number of Presbyterian clergy at Yale.

Taylor had joined the faculty at Yale in 1822 and developed a distinctive 'New Haven Theology' that questioned traditional Calvinism. 'Taylorism' questioned the historic understanding of original sin, calling it an irrational belief, and redefined regeneration as the voluntary change of the governing principle of a person's life. This view was opposed to traditional Calvinism, which understood regeneration as the divine creation of a new disposition. Taylor claimed to be an orthodox Calvinist, but there was grave concern that he had moved dangerously close to 'Pelagianism' — a fourth-century heresy which denied original sin, claiming that human beings have full freedom of choice to obey God because there was no sin nature passed on to posterity.

The Princeton professors wrote numerous essays contesting this new theology. Archibald Alexander weighed in on Taylor's views in an 1830 *Biblical Repertory* article which raised the specter of the Pelagian heresy. Yale pushed back, publishing several essays defending Taylor's views. Hodge entered the dispute at this point, writing that he was concerned about where New Haven ideas might be headed. For Hodge, denying the imputation of Adam's sin to posterity was dangerous because, according to St Paul, the imputation of Christ's righteousness to the sinner was inseparably connected to the imputation of Adam's sin. As Hodge indicated, history warned that after a first step, a teacher's disciples often took the second step. How pervasive was

# The great schism

this theology in the Presbyterian Church? This was a much-contested question. Hodge wrote that it was 'inconsiderate as to numbers', but this view was not shared by some Old School conservatives. Fears about Taylorism intensified as his theology became identified with revivalism.

Much of the ongoing doctrinal dispute between the two parties concerned the question of confessional subscription. Conservative Old School advocates, convinced that lenient New School Presbyterians were unwilling to discipline unorthodox ministers, argued for a strict standard of subscription to the *Westminster Confession* (1646) as the cure. The religious periodicals of the time were filled with debate over the meaning of confessional subscription. During his tenure as a Princeton professor, Hodge was repeatedly called upon to weigh in on the old question of ministerial subscription to the *Westminster Confession of Faith*.

American Presbyterians had adopted the *Westminster Confession of Faith* as a doctrinal standard as early as 1729, but there had been ongoing dispute for one hundred years over the meaning of clergy subscription to the confession of faith. Hodge first entered the current debate on confessional subscription in an 1831 article in the *Biblical Repertory*. The Presbyterian ordination vow (1788) had stated, 'Do you sincerely receive and adopt the confession of faith of this church as containing the system of doctrine taught in the Holy Scriptures?' What did it mean for a minister to subscribe to the confession's 'system of doctrine'? Hodge said that there were two extreme answers to the question which should be avoided — one was too severe, the other too lax.

Hodge argued for a median position which understood 'system of doctrine' to refer to the essential doctrines of Calvinism that were distinctive in the *Westminster Confession*; that is, the 'Calvinistic system' of doctrine. His view was opposed to both an overly strict position, which expected ministers to embrace all the doctrines of the confession, and the latitudinarian position that only required subscription to 'the great fundamental doctrines of the gospel'. Hodge claimed that a strict view was impractical, because a large number of ministers cannot all be expected to hold identical views concerning such a large document as the *Westminster Confession of Faith*. On the other hand, the broader view would be dishonest, because a church which professed particular beliefs should indeed hold them. Of course, there was diversity of doctrinal opinion, but certain doctrines uniquely define Reformed theology, and Presbyterian ministers should be expected to teach this essential Calvinism.

As the theological conflict unfolded, it became clear that there was a continuum of opinion within each party; there was no monolithic Old School camp, nor was there absolute unanimity on the New School side. Hodge and his fellow Princeton professors represented a group of moderate Old School men who accepted most New School Presbyterians as orthodox. The Princeton 'peace men' (as they were called) appealed to the larger church for a balanced perspective. Each party contained a moderate middle that agreed with the Princeton professors, but vocal minorities often tried to drown them out.

Old School conservatives decided to take matters into their own hands by attacking particular New School clergy. Albert

Barnes, pastor of First Presbyterian Church in Philadelphia, had charges filed against him in 1831 for the content of his sermon, 'The Way of Salvation'. Complaints were raised about receiving Barnes (a Princeton graduate) into Philadelphia Presbytery. Neither presbytery nor synod could resolve the issue, so it was appealed to the General Assembly. The case was referred to a committee, chaired by Hodge's colleague Dr Samuel Miller of Princeton, which recommended that all proceedings against Mr Barnes be suspended. The General Assembly concurred. Not satisfied with this outcome, Old School conservatives would continually press their agenda at annual General Assembly meetings during the 1830s.

Another focal point of Old School/New School dissension was revivalism, especially the ministry of Charles G. Finney from New York. Finney was pursuing the study of law when he had a dramatic conversion experience and sensed God's call to become an evangelist in 1821. After being tutored by a Presbyterian mentor, the Rev. George Gale, he was ordained as a Presbyterian minister in July 1824. Commissioned as a missionary to upstate New York by the Female Missionary Society of the Western District, he began his controversial preaching career in the 1824 revivals in Jefferson and St Lawrence Counties. Finney's preaching immediately yielded a harvest of souls in a number of small villages as well as the towns of Troy, Utica, Rome (Oneida County), and Auburn. These 'Western Revivals' were the scenes of Finney's experiments with new methods of revivalism which would attract much protest from conservatives. The so-called 'new measures' of Finney included his preaching style and innovations such as the 'anxious seat', protracted meetings, particular prayer, the 'prayer of faith', and allowing women to pray and exhort in public meetings. Before Finney's work in New York, earlier revivals had taken place within the churches under the preaching of parish pastors. Finney's itinerant ministry inaugurated a new approach to revival ministry in upstate New York.

Hodge and his Princeton colleagues were concerned about Finney, but cautious about speaking out against him. Finney caused quite a stir with his sermon, 'Sinners Bound to Change Their Own Hearts', preached at the Congregational Park Street Church in Boston in the fall of 1831. Finney asserted that while God influences the sinner to turn towards him, it is actually the sinner who is the primary author of changing his own heart and coming to God. There was an outcry against the sermon by Calvinists and a push back by Finney supporters. The contents of the sermon became public knowledge through a critical pamphlet, 'The New Divinity Tried', authored by a minister who had taken copious notes during the sermon. An anonymous rebuttal in print which supported Finney then appeared. Hodge decided to weigh in on the controversy in the *Biblical Repertory* with an 1832 article: 'The New Divinity Tried; or An Examination of the Rev. Rand's Strictures on a Sermon delivered by the Rev. C. G. Finney on Making a New Heart'.

Fair-minded Hodge began his article by admitting the impropriety of Mr Rand presenting Finney's views on the basis of his own notes from an extemporaneous sermon without Finney's input first. Nevertheless, since the friends of Finney had responded to Rand in writing, it was then appropriate for him to offer his views. The defense of Finney had included a litany of quotations from prominent

Calvinist theologians whom the author suggested would be supportive of Finney's views. Hodge spent significant time debunking this assertion with his own series of quotations from these divines, showing that 'Every one of these writers not only disclaims the opinion thus ascribed to them, but endeavors to refute it.'

Hodge charged Finney and those who preached similar messages with denying the doctrine of original sin in their assertion that the sinner is only to make a choice for God apart from reference to the enabling power of the Holy Spirit and the cross of Christ. This is 'another gospel' when conviction of sin and the cross are kept out of view. Thankfully, the Spirit of God works despite these errors as persons peruse the Scripture and 'feel the need of the Savior and go to him as the gospel directs'; thus the 'lamentable neglect of the grand doctrines of the gospel is prevented'. Hodge clarified that he did not doubt that these preachers, if asked, would deny intending to leave Christ out; but their manner in press and pulpit was defective in presenting the biblical mode of salvation.

Presbyterian support for revivalism was strongest among the New School ranks. The heart of the debate was over evangelistic methodology. How would Presbyterians present the gospel to the spiritually destitute of America? Theological controversies were a subsidiary concern of the overarching concern for lost souls. False conversions were rampant in these revivals as far as some of the Old School men were concerned. Many Old Schoolers were convinced that revivalist errors were dangerous and produced easy conversions which were contrived and would fade with time. New School advocates, on the other hand, believed that a great harvest of souls was at hand, and that to oppose this was resisting God's work of revival. This was a personal, deeply-felt issue, as the souls of men were at stake, and few held dispassionate opinions.

The strict Old School party, outraged by the toleration of revivalist errors, began publishing dissent papers. These protests were an attempt to herald specific ecclesiastical and theological concerns, with the aim of recruiting Old School moderates against the New School. The first of these protest documents came before the 1834 Assembly and was known as the 'Western Memorial'. The conservatives listed numerous doctrinal innovations on imputation, ability, and the atonement 'which are held and taught within the Presbyterian Church, which the General Assembly are constitutionally competent to suppress'. Albert Barnes, Lyman Beecher, George Duffield, and Nathaniel S. S. Beman were implicated by name as primary sources of New School errors. The memorial called the church to censor these doctrinal aberrations and faithfully deal with the cases that were referred to the General Assembly. The 1834 Assembly did not concur with the judgement of the Western Memorial and reprimanded its advocates for publicly defaming ministers without trial.

Undeterred, Old School conservatives, dissatisfied with the 1834 General Assembly's unwillingness to condemn New School errors, decided to enlist the aid of Dr Hodge for a revised statement they called the 'Act and Testimony'. He reluctantly gave input because of his concern that previous lists of errors were about peripheral issues and not fundamental theological errors. As an example of legitimate doctrinal diversity, Hodge asked, 'Is it to be expected that, at this time of the day, the Assembly would condemn all who do not hold to the doctrine of a limited atonement?' With Hodge's assistance the new document focused on the errors of Taylorism.

The final published version of the Act and Testimony had three sections: doctrine, discipline, and recommendations to the church. Reaction to the Act and Testimony at Princeton was not what conservatives had planned. Hodge came out against the Act and Testimony in the *Biblical Repertory*, stating that he believed that only a small minority of the church would support it. Rather than a legitimate testimony against error, 'the signing of the Testimony as a test of orthodoxy' was being proposed; this would bring division to the Presbyterian Church. The Act and Testimony asserted that doctrinal errors 'are held and taught by many persons in our church'. Hodge disagreed, countering, 'We have not the least idea, that one-tenth of the ministers of the Presbyterian Church would deliberately countenance and sustain the errors specified.' He wrote:

> So long as the standards of any church remain unaltered, its members profess the same faith which they avowed when they joined it. I do not profess to hold or to teach what A. B. or C. may be known to believe, but I profess to believe the confession of faith of the church to which I belong. It matters not, therefore, so far as this point is concerned how corrupt a portion, or even the majority, of the church may be, provided I am not called upon to profess their errors. Instead of my mere ecclesiastical connexion with them being a countenancing of their errors, it may give me the best opportunity of constantly testifying against them.

Archibald Alexander admitted that Princeton professors found themselves in the middle, but he defended Princeton's stance, 'Our opinions and feelings did not entirely coincide with EITHER CLASS of the ultra partisans who have, for several years past, divided and agitated our church.' Could Princeton stand by silently and 'see our beloved church torn in pieces by honest, but misguided friends, on the one hand, and a really small hostile junto on the other, without lifting a hand or voice to stay the catastrophe?' Princeton opposed the Act and Testimony because she was 'persuaded that nine-tenths of our ministry are in great measure free from the unsound opinions in question. We believe, moreover, that the errors to which reference is here made, are declining rather than gaining ground.' Alexander urged Presbyterians to stop fighting each other. Instead they should 'have but one matter of strife — namely, who shall love the Master most, and who shall serve him with the greatest zeal.'

While ecclesiastical tempests were churning among Presbyterians, the national debate over slavery was heating up and overflowing into the church. The American slavery situation had become intense by the 1830s. Radical abolitionist papers like William Lloyd Garrison's *The Liberator*, Nat Turner's massacre of fifty-seven whites in Virginia, and rumors of more slave uprisings had produced a hardened pro-slavery attitude in the South. Presbyterians struggled in the prolonged contest over black slavery just like all the other American denominations.

In 1818 the Presbyterian Church had adopted a very strong anti-slavery statement written by Princeton Seminary board president, Ashbel Green. The Presbyterians declared, 'We consider the voluntary enslaving of one part of the human race by another, as a gross violation of the most precious and sacred rights of human nature; as utterly inconsistent with the laws of God, which requires us to love our neighbor as ourselves, and as totally irreconcilable with the spirit and principles of the gospel of Christ...' While condemning slavery, the statement recognized the particular difficulties of the South with her inherited situation.

This moderate policy kept the slavery topic at bay in Assembly deliberations until 1835, when an overture from Ohio reintroduced the subject, eliciting a predictable Southern reaction. The incendiary nature of the overture, calling on the church to remove the evils of slavery, ignited Southern Presbyterian passions. Advocates of immediate abolition, very visible at the 1835 General Assembly, vexed Southerners accustomed to Presbyterian toleration of slaveholding. For the first time since 1818, the General Assembly commissioned a full study of the slavery question. Princeton professor Samuel Miller was selected as chair of the Committee on Slavery which would report back to the 1836 Assembly.

Nothing provoked theological tempers like debate over the prudence of abolition. The revival movements under Finney and his disciples had initiated a renewal of anti-slavery agitation in the North. The abolitionist cause became increasingly identified with the New School, since radical abolitionist rhetoric was strongest in regions where the New School predominated. The Princeton professors, as well as Old School conservatives, were agreed in their opposition to allowing abolitionist agitation into the Presbyterian Church. Southern synods reiterated their position that the General Assembly had no constitutional authority to legislate on slavery.

Charles Hodge endeared himself to Southerners in an April 1836 article in the *Biblical Repertory*. In a review of Unitarian minister William Ellery Channing's book *Slavery* (1835), Hodge argued that since the Bible does not condemn slavery, 'slaveholding is not necessarily sinful.' He also rebuked the abolition movement for declaring slaveholding a crime. He concluded, 'The great duty of the South is not emancipation, but improvement.' In the same month, the Presbytery of New Brunswick, where the Princeton professors held membership, adopted a resolution declaring that the church had no right to interfere with the civil relation between master and slave.

Meanwhile, Albert Barnes again became the target of Old School conservatives. In 1835 Barnes had published a commentary on the book of Romans, which he had intended as a Sunday School resource. Immediately, Old School papers and periodicals began attacking Barnes' *Notes on Romans* as 'unsound and dangerous'. Charles Hodge offered a balanced review. While acknowledging that there were some erroneous statements, he contended that there was much good in the book, and that Barnes was not a heretic. Conservatives, determined to prosecute Barnes a second time, brought charges against him for doctrines 'contrary to the Standards of the Presbyterian Church'. Barnes was acquitted by his presbytery in the summer of 1835, but when Synod reversed this decision and suspended him from the ministry, Barnes appealed to the General Assembly. Conservatives viewed the Barnes case coming before the 1836 Assembly as a referendum on New School doctrine that would determine the fate of the Presbyterian Church.

# The great schism

By 1836 it appeared that schism between the Old School and New School parties in the Presbyterian Church was inevitable. The New School also viewed the upcoming Assembly as a test case for confessional boundaries in the Presbyterian Church. Determined to exonerate Barnes, whose convictions were shared by a number of New School men, the New School was irritated by the censorious spirit of Barnes' Old School attackers and was in no mood to negotiate. The 1836 New School majority pushed through their agenda on Barnes and slavery, completely alienating Old School conservatives by their unwillingness to compromise at any point. The General Assembly of 1836 cleared Barnes of all charges, refusing to censure any of his writings. Dr Miller tried to broker a moderate concession by proposing at least censuring some portions of Barnes' commentary, but Miller's attempt to offer the Old School an olive branch failed. On the slavery question, a motion to 'indefinitely postpone' any discussion passed, but vociferous New School protests against postponement sealed in the Southern mind a connection of abolition with New Schoolism.

As soon as the 1836 General Assembly concluded, Old School leaders began to organize for a response. The strict Old School men were convinced that ecclesiastical separation from the New School was the only option left, since discipline in church courts had failed. Hodge was dismayed by New School unwillingness to find middle ground, but he firmly asserted that there were still insufficient grounds to justify a schism. Princeton's influence was waning, and her pleas for peace went unheeded by resolute Old School conservatives who urged Princeton to get on board for an inevitable split.

In 1837 Old School conservatives held a pre-Assembly Convention. They adopted a hands-off strategy on slavery and issued a declaration on the problems in the church: 'hostility to the doctrines of the confession', toleration of the 'heresies of Taylor', and the 'policies of Finney'. According to the Old School convention, all of these errors were 'virtually sanctioned' by the 1836 Assembly. When the 1837 General Assembly convened, an Old School moderator was elected in a close ballot. The Old School then proceeded to systematically dismantle the denomination by exscinding four New School synods and ordering the investigation of errors in several presbyteries. After the Assembly had finished its ecclesiastical surgery, all under loud New School protests, the New School members of the Assembly reconvened the next day at Albert Barnes' church. The New School challenged the accusations of heresy and condemned the Assembly's 'unconstitutional measures', directing all New School presbyteries to send delegates to the 1838 Assembly the next year. When the 1838 General Assembly opened, New School commissioners from the four excluded synods were not recognized, so these delegates and those from twenty-nine other New School presbyteries elected their own Assembly officers and adjourned to another location.

Hodge and his colleagues had made intensive efforts in the 1830s to salvage the unity of the Presbyterian Church, but by 1838 there were two separate denominations. The Princeton men, though peacemakers, were clearly Old School in orientation and after the schism fully supported their distinctive Old School church. Immediately following the split, Hodge spent three years (1838–1841) writing his two-volume *Constitutional History of the Presbyterian Church in the United States*, in part to vindicate the Old School party as the legitimate heirs of historic Presbyterianism. In the *History*, Hodge revisited the subscription issue and rehearsed the story of the 1729 Adopting Act as well as later colonial Presbyterian history to establish his argument that Old School views of subscription had historic precedent in the church.

The second volume of Hodge's *History* began with an account of the eighteenth-century First Great Awakening (1740s) and the attendant problems with the emotional excess associated with the revival. The pro-revival New Side Presbyterians had been guilty of participating in some of the extreme behavior produced by the revival preachers. Nonetheless, Hodge wrote about the need for revival during this era because of a pervasive spiritual coldness in America and a dearth of 'experimental religion' among the clergy. There were genuine conversions under Whitefield's preaching, but Hodge claimed that there were also spurious emotional experiences resulting from nervous disorders. Whitefield's dramatic descriptions of hell, for example, stirred the passions, producing outbursts of emotion and bodily agitations, such as hysterical crying and fainting. Hodge argued that these outward manifestations did not accompany the preaching of Christ and the apostles recorded in Scripture.

Hodge also criticized Jonathan Edwards for allowing the emotional outbursts that were part of the revival in Northampton. Even though Edwards clarified that these behaviors were not inherently evidence of genuine religious affections, he still did not exercise sufficient caution in allowing these things to continue under his ministry. Hodge asked: if these things occurred under Edwards, who was known for his piety and judgement, what about others who were not nearly as discerning as Edwards? He also indicated that something must have been askew in the Northampton revival, for afterwards religion in this area declined.

Hodge's criteria for evaluating genuine revival included several factors: Are the doctrines preached the central doctrines of the Christian faith (such as original sin, regeneration, justification, faith, and repentance)? What kind of experience is evident? Do the converts experience conviction of sin, dependence on Christ for salvation and a desire to live an obedient life before God? Lastly, what are the actual effects of the awakening on people's lives? These factors were all important to Hodge, because he had personally witnessed the shallowness of nineteenth-century revivals which, from his perspective, had borne little fruit.

Not all of Hodge's colleagues at Princeton agreed with his negative analysis of the eighteenth-century awakening. Archibald Alexander, who lectured to Princeton students about revivals, wrote a history of the 'Log College' and its graduates (1851) which extolled the eighteenth-century Presbyterian revivalists for infusing a new spirit into the colonial church. Hodge later seemed to modify his views about the Great Awakening, writing about the 'extraordinary power' of the Holy Spirit that appeared during the revival, producing a 'saving knowledge of the truth and a high degree of spiritual life' among the people. Princeton, like much of the Presbyterian Church, held conflicting views about revivals but always rejoiced at the testimonies of those genuinely converted to Christ.

# 4

## SEMINARY LIFE

In 1840, the General Assembly of the Old School church elected Hodge to the chair of Exegetical and Didactic Theology, the post which had been held by Archibald Alexander, who was now sixty-eight. For the next few years, Alexander and Hodge would co-teach the theology courses as Hodge transitioned into being the primary theology professor at the seminary. Alexander's new title was Professor of Pastoral and Polemic Theology, which he would hold to the end of his life. While Hodge was reluctant to move into this position, he agreed to take on the new responsibility in deference to Alexander's wishes. He was now forty-three years old, and it would be as theology professor for the next three decades that he would make his lasting mark on the seminary and the church. Teaching Bible courses in the original languages since his mid-twenties had amply prepared him for this next phase of his teaching career. For Hodge, systematic theology was simply the organization of the biblical material into logical topics; thus it was a fairly smooth transition into this new focus for his lectures.

Hodge's lectures, known for their insightful clarity, were read to students, some of whom took extensive notes and made copies of the lectures for future students. This became frustrating to Hodge, who observed the students' waning interest in lectures since they already possessed a transcript of his presentations. It had been his habit to require students to write out answers to questions he provided; but with his notes in hand, they simply transcribed Hodge's material from notes rather than write their own thoughtful answers. His preferred method of teaching became oral examination, which energized the students, pushing them to master material rather than just relying on his lecture notes.

Alumni of the seminary remembered Dr Hodge as kind and fatherly in his classroom demeanor, with a keen intellect that challenged the students to think. One of Hodge's most famous students was Benjamin Breckinridge Warfield who would himself later become a theology professor at Western Seminary, Pittsburgh (1878–1887), before joining the Princeton faculty. After his student years at Princeton Seminary, B. B. Warfield studied with prominent professors in Europe, but Hodge remained his role model as a teacher. Professor Warfield wrote,

> I have sat under many noted teachers, and yet am free to say that as an educator I consider Dr Hodge superior to them all. He was in fact my ideal of a teacher. Best of all men I have ever known, he knew how to make a young man think ... I cannot hope either to describe this mode of teaching or express my profound admiration for it. I can only say that in that room of Systematic Theology, I think I had daily before me examples of perfect teaching. The way he managed his

# Seminary life

*own accumulations of learning too — constantly drawing on them for illustration and enforcement, constantly the master of them, and of every detail of them, was marvelous ... Every jot of that learning, consecrated to the Master's cause, was ready to be utilized in the recitation room. Every jot of it was Christianized by its passage through his mind from whatever source it was drawn. Had I never gained another thing at Princeton, I would bless God for permitting me to see this!*

Another former student, who also taught at Western Seminary, wrote to Hodge seeking his advice on how best to instruct students. Hodge wrote back to Dr William S. Plumer describing his balanced approach of lectures, questioning and writing, humbly acknowledging what he perceived to be weaknesses in his own method. In response to a question about what resources had been most helpful to him as a professor, he replied, 'I have read, generally, everything I could on each topic, orthodox and heterodox, and got what good I could from each. Turretine's *Institutes* I regard as incomparably the best book as a whole on systematic theology...' This work, the primary text Hodge assigned in his theology classes, was written in Latin by the seventeenth-century Swiss theologian Francis Turretin.

In addition to theological instruction, Hodge labored to teach the students about genuine Christian piety, a pattern that Alexander had established at Princeton from the beginning. A central element of seminary life for all faculty and students was the 'Sabbath Afternoon Conference', when faculty and seminarians would meet to discuss 'experimental religion'. The Sunday conference was a time of reflection on one's personal walk with God and encouraging one another in a life of devotion to Christ. A week beforehand the Sunday afternoon topic would be announced to the students, who would come prepared to discuss a theme in practical Christian living such as prayer, fasting, imitation of Christ, the Great Commission, etc. The meeting would begin with prayer and singing, after which a student would initiate the discussion, followed by Alexander unfolding his own experience and insights.

All the professors participated in the Sunday conferences, with Hodge as the prominent speaker after Dr Alexander died. Hodge would typically come prepared with messages to present on Sunday afternoons. Where Alexander had tended to focus solely on practical subjects, Hodge expanded his talks to include doctrinal as well as practical topics; but always directing the conversation towards the practical nature of all Christian doctrine. Students were deeply moved by these fervent presentations directed toward personal spiritual experience. One graduate remarked about Hodge's Sunday messages, 'No triumph of his with tongue or pen ever so thrilled and moved human hearts as did his utterances at the Sabbath afternoon conferences in the seminary Oratory, which will live in the immortal memory of every Princeton student.'

A. A. Hodge, a Princeton student in the 1840s, wrote that the Sunday conferences were 'in many respects the most remarkable and memorable exercise in the entire Seminary course'. In the weekly exercise, 'The dry and cold attributes of scientific theology moving in the sphere of the intellect, gave place to the warmth of personal religious experience.'

He added, 'Here in the most effective manner they sought to build up Christian men rather than form accomplished scholars and to instruct them in the wisest method of conducting their future work of saving souls and edifying the Church of Christ.' After Charles Hodge's death, one of his former pupils wrote, 'Far above his fame as a champion of truth, was and is his glory that he gloried in the Cross of Christ. He was a child-like, humble, praying, believing, hoping Christian. In the Oratory on Sunday afternoons his spiritual "talks" to the students were like streams of the water of life flowing by the throne!'

Hodge was always interested in drawing students' attention to the practical implications of all theology, having imbibed this practice from his mentor, Archibald Alexander. At Princeton Alexander had attempted to steer a middle way between an overemphasis on objective doctrinal correctness as the essence of Christianity and an exclusively subjective emotionalism often associated with some forms of revivalism. There was another option, a more biblical one according to Alexander, where head and heart each played their legitimate role in Christian faith. Neither lifeless intellectualism nor religious feelings alone constituted the essence of true Christian conversion, but a union of genuine pious affections and orthodox theology. Hodge reiterated this same motif in his writings on the meaning of Christian piety. For Hodge, Scripture was key to understanding the Christian experience; for not only does the Word of God teach one about Christ and salvation, but it also provides a test of valid Christian experience through stories of changed lives recorded in Scripture.

The fusion of head and heart was also evident in Hodge's writing. One of his most well-known books was the popularly accessible, *The Way of Life*. The American Sunday School Union had asked Professor Hodge to write a book for 'intelligent and educated young persons', and he obliged by writing *The Way of Life*, published in 1841. It has been characterized as a layman's version of his later *Systematic Theology*, because it was heavy on Christian doctrine. As stated in the introduction, the basic outline of the book was simple: Are the Scriptures from God? If so, what do they teach? And how should these truths affect the way one lives? The book became very popular, with strong affirmation among the Christian public.

Hodge began *The Way of Life* by discussing the divine origin of the Bible. His emphasis was upon the inner witness of God's truth for a believer who encountered God's moral requirements in the Word of God. These biblical demands touch a person's moral nature and point to the divine origin of Scripture. In addition, the person and character of Christ revealed in the Bible are a manifestation of God's glory and a testimony to its truthfulness. Hodge drew a parallel between the revelation of God's perfections in nature and the manifestation of his authority in the pages of Scripture. Thus, the Christian experienced God's truth in the reading of the Bible. Hodge pointed out that many Christians believed the Bible for the same reasons they believed in God, 'because they see his glory and feel his authority and power'.

A Christian's subjective feelings were tied to objective reality, as Hodge demonstrated in his review of basic Christian doctrines in *The Way of Life*. The inner peace and joy a believer experienced was produced by the objective reality of what Christ has done to reconcile believers to God the Father. The ground of certainty in the Christian life was Christ's work of reconciliation, not mere subjective feelings. According to Hodge, Christian experience confirmed true doctrine, but the objective foundation of God's salvation through Christ must be primary.

In the final sections of *The Way of Life*, Hodge wrote about the Christian's growth in holiness through progressive sanctification. The obedience one offered to God was not mere outward duty but was rooted in communion with God as the loving father of his children. This communion was experienced in private and public worship, which produced great joy in the believer's heart. The renewed soul was invigorated by the Spirit 'to make it active in the service and praise of God'. The means by which the life of God in the soul was maintained and promoted was communication with the Holy Spirit through prayer. Flowing from this communion, one pursued religious duty by meditating on the Word of God, ingraining the truth in one's mind. The Christian life gave evidence of progress as the soul conformed to God and performed its duty before him.

Hodge consistently maintained this understanding of the Christian faith throughout his years as a professor. Two decades later, in an 1860 article, 'What is Christianity?', Hodge defined faith as 'both a doctrine and a life'. Objectively, Christianity was God's testimony about man's redemption through Christ contained in the Scriptures; subjectively, 'It is the life of Christ in the soul ... which is due to the indwelling of his Spirit.' Another way he described it was the philosophical and religious conception of God (mind and heart), and 'In the Bible both elements are harmonized; though the latter is the predominant, as it should be with us.' For Charles Hodge, the objective and subjective aspects of Christianity were inseparable.

A principal component of Christian piety for Princetonians was the Great Commission. The seminary had been established as a 'nursery for missionaries to the heathen', according to the 1811 'Plan of the Seminary' adopted by the Presbyterian General Assembly. Alexander had set the missionary tone at Princeton, stating, 'we regard the missionary cause as the greatest beneath the sun'. Two years after the seminary opened, students had organized the 'Society of Inquiry on Missions and the General State of Religion' in 1814. Students preparing for missionary service or with a keen interest in missions at home and abroad gathered on the first day of each month to hear information on revivals and missions and letters from missionaries, or to discuss a missions-related topic. Princeton students corresponded with similar organizations at other colleges and seminaries as well as writing letters to missionaries on the field such as Baptist missionary pioneer William Carey in India. The Society of Inquiry at Princeton was part of a larger student missionary movement that swept across America in the first half of the nineteenth century. The fruit of Princeton's embrace of the Great Commission was the fact that one-third of the graduates during the first fifty years served on the mission field.

Hodge's personal zeal for missions was kindled when he heard one of William Carey's colleagues, William Ward, speak at the seminary in 1821 just as he was beginning his teaching responsibilities at Princeton. Writing to his brother Hugh the next day, he confided, 'Looking at these men in India, giving the Bible to so many millions, which I know can never be in vain, I see them opening a perennial fountain, which, when they are dead for ages, will still afford eternal life to millions. Should we die, which of our works would we wish to follow us?' Hodge never seemed to waiver from this conviction that mission service was among the highest of callings, addressing this theme regularly in his teaching and preaching. By the 1840s, Hodge was actively serving on the Presbyterian Board of Foreign Missions and the Board of Domestic Missions, remaining a member of the Domestic Board until 1870. In May 1848, he preached a sermon on Matthew 28:19-20 for the Presbyterian Board of Foreign Missions which was published by the Board in their annual report for that year.

During the prime of his teaching career in his fifties, Hodge witnessed a series of deaths within a few short years that brought much sadness to his life. In September 1849, his wife Sarah became very ill, and though the doctors predicted her recovery, she died within three months. All of her children, with the exception of her oldest, were at her side in those last days of her earthly life. Her husband described her as 'sweetly humble and resigned'. She expressed confidence in her salvation through Christ as she approached death and said of her children, 'I give them to God.' She passed away early in the morning on Christmas Day. Charles was heartbroken to lose his beloved wife of twenty-seven years. He had inscribed on her tombstone these words: 'We lay you gently here, our best beloved, to gather strength and beauty for the coming of the Lord.'

A year later, his brother Hugh lost a seventeen-year-old son to disease. Charles, writing out of his own experience of loss, wrote to his brother, 'There is no help in such afflictions but in God. He alone can reach the heart. Earthly friends speak only to the outward ear ... It was never meant that we should not sorrow after the most cherished objects of our affection ... The great means of having our sorrow kept pure is to keep near to God, to feel assured of his love, that he orders all things well, and will make even our afflictions work out for us a far more exceeding and an eternal weight of glory.'

Hodge's colleague, Samuel Miller, died on 7 January 1850. Miller was the second professor at Princeton, joining Alexander on the faculty in 1813. He had been one of Hodge's professors when he was a seminary student and then his colleague on the faculty for almost three decades. Miller served a Presbyterian pastorate in New York before moving to the seminary to become Professor of Ecclesiastical History and Church Government. Miller was a historian distinguished for his advocacy of Presbyterian doctrine and form of government. Hodge had lost someone he highly respected for his contribution to the seminary and exemplary Christian character. When Dr Miller died, Hodge replaced him as a Trustee of the College of New Jersey, serving his *alma mater* faithfully for the next twenty-seven years. His connection to the college, so significant in his own intellectual development and Christian conversion, always remained close to his heart.

Less than two years after the death of Dr Miller, Hodge would also lose his beloved mentor, Archibald Alexander. Having put all his earthly affairs in order during his final days,

Alexander summoned Hodge to his bedside to say goodbye. In a letter to his brother three days later, Hodge recalled the parting words of his mentor: 'I consider it one of my greatest blessings that I have been able to bring you forward, and now, my dear son, farewell.' Then he related his own feelings: 'It is forty years next spring since I first, as a boy, attracted his notice. He has ever since acted to me as a father, and God has given me grace to love and revere him as a child would such a father.' Within a week Dr Alexander left this world on 22 October 1851 and was buried in the graveyard on Witherspoon Street two days later. During the funeral procession, Charles Hodge accompanied the coffin along with Alexander's six sons. With Drs Miller and Alexander deceased, Hodge was now the senior member of the faculty and would be singularly responsible for continuing the Princeton tradition.

Amidst his earthly sorrow, God providentially provided a new wife for Charles Hodge. The bride was Mary Hunter Stockton, whom he had known for many years. She had been a close friend of his first wife Sarah and fitted in with the Hodge children easily because they already knew her. Mary was the widow of Samuel Stockton, a naval officer; her father was a Presbyterian clergyman. On 8 July 1852 Charles and Mary became husband and wife. A. A. Hodge remembered his stepmother as a noble Christian woman who did an exemplary job raising his younger siblings and taking care of his father.

Caring for the children was a labor Hodge took seriously as a father, and he was grateful for a second helpmate who ably assisted him in the task. He had written on this topic a few years before in a review of Horace Bushnell's book, *Christian Nurture* (1847). Bushnell, pastor of the North (Congregational) Church in Hartford, Connecticut, had studied under Nathaniel Taylor at Yale Divinity School in the 1830s. In *Christian Nurture* Bushnell proposed a non-revivalist approach to Christianity where a child gradually grew as a Christian through deliberate means of training by parents and the church. Hodge agreed with Bushnell's approach, which emphasized the 'ordinary means of grace' rather than dependence on revivals, which may produce a false faith leading persons 'to think that piety consists in strong exercise of feelings'. According to Hodge, God worked through 'the divinely appointed means of careful Christian nurture.'

While praising Bushnell for his insights, Hodge indicated that the shortcoming of the book was its attributing all Christian growth to a natural human process without proper acknowledgment of the work of the Spirit. For Hodge, parental training of children may be a means God uses for the salvation of children, but it was God who granted repentance and faith to the individual. No doubt Hodge's own childhood experience of his mother's instruction and prayers influenced his own thinking on these matters. He viewed the spiritual training of children as a part of the covenantal structure of the Christian family reflected in God's covenant with Abraham and his descendants. Christianity was not something 'natural', but believers were 'raised from spiritual death and so united to Christ as to become partakers of his life', which was maintained by the constant indwelling of the Spirit.

Investing himself in his children's lives paid significant dividends in the years and generations to come. Two of Charles Hodge's sons would teach at the seminary alongside their father, and one grandson, Caspar Wistar Jr, would be a professor of systematic theology at the seminary from 1921 until his death in 1937. The first child to join the senior Hodge on the faculty was Caspar Wistar Hodge (1830–1891), who moved back to Princeton in 1860, at the age of thirty, to begin his teaching career. Caspar Hodge was a gifted student, finishing at the head of his class at the College of New Jersey in 1848. He possessed unique skill in Greek and became a Greek tutor at the college after his graduation. Young Hodge eventually pursued a divinity degree at Princeton Seminary, graduating in 1853 and then worked as a pastor serving congregations in New York and Pennsylvania. When a faculty vacancy opened at the seminary, Caspar's name surfaced as a likely candidate. His father believed he had the gifts for the task but probably not the interest; nonetheless, the younger Hodge decided to accept a teaching position at his *alma mater*.

In 1860 the Presbyterian General Assembly elected Caspar Wistar Hodge to the chair of New Testament Literature and Exegesis, where he served for thirty-one years. Teaching New Testament courses, including Greek, he methodically read lectures to students on the books of the New Testament, the canon, the life of Christ, and the history of the apostolic church. He did not publish books like his father, but was known for classroom skill in exegesis of the biblical text. The students remembered him fondly for inspiring them to careful biblical study.

There were three Hodges at Princeton during this period; Caspar's youngest brother, Francis Blanchard Hodge, was a twenty-two-year-old seminary student at the time. Francis Hodge, the youngest of the five Hodge boys, was born in 1838, and like his older brothers attended both the College of New Jersey and the seminary. After ordination to the Presbyterian ministry, Francis received a call as pastor of the Presbyterian Church in Oxford, Pennsylvania, one of the congregations his brother Caspar had previously served. In 1869 he moved to the First Presbyterian Church in Wilkesbarre, Pennsylvania, serving this congregation for fourteen years. The eldest son, Archibald Alexander, had been pastor of the Wilkesbarre church from 1861–1864. Apparently these two congregations appreciated having a Hodge as pastor. A. A. Hodge would also later serve on the Princeton faculty with his brother Casper and his father. The Hodge family name was a prominent fixture at Princeton Seminary for a long time.

In addition to his teaching responsibilities at the seminary, Hodge found time to engage the burning issues of the day, in both church and state, through the pages of the *Biblical Repertory*. The 1840s and 50s were a period of American national expansion — statehood for Texas in 1845, the California gold rush, and the Oregon territory coming under United States jurisdiction. The nation was at war with Mexico (1848), and fresh waves of immigrants from Ireland, Germany, and China came to America during this period. Presbyterians built churches and mission stations across the newly-populated territories. These included the first Chinese Presbyterian Church, which was organized in California in 1853. By mid-century, Presbyterian churches

# Seminary life

had been planted across the nation, and established churches were giving faithfully to support home missions. These were exciting days for home missions; but it was also a tense era because of the vexing dilemma of slavery in the states.

Sectional strain between slave and free states increased as vocal anti-slavery men continued their unabated attack upon the South, and Southerners pushed back with hardened pro-slavery positions. The Fugitive Slave Act of 1850, the publishing of *Uncle Tom's Cabin* in 1851 (by Harriet Beecher Stowe, daughter of New School Minister, Lyman Beecher), and the 1857 Dred Scott decision each added to the swelling crisis. The 1850s' mayhem in 'bleeding Kansas' became an armed contest between pro-slavery and anti-slavery settlers. Militant abolitionist John Brown and six companions executed five pro-slavery Kansas settlers in 1856. In 1859 Brown tried to initiate a slave insurrection at Harper's Ferry, Virginia, but was stopped by soldiers under Colonel Robert E. Lee. The whole nation was preoccupied with the status of America's peculiar institution. The church was in no position to escape unscathed from this pervasive problem which divided Christians as well as other citizens. Hodge engaged the slave debate on numerous occasions in the *Biblical Repertory*. In an October 1849 article, 'Emancipation', Hodge offered a comprehensive account of his personal views:

> *The question is not about the continuance of slavery and of the present system, but about the proper method of effecting the removal of the evil. We maintain, that it is not by denouncing slaveholding as a sin, or by universal agitation at the North, but by the improvement of the slaves ... We hold it to be the grand principle of the gospel, that every man*

> *is bound to promote the moral, intellectual, and physical improvement of his fellow men ... We think, therefore, that the true method for Christians to treat this subject, is to follow the example of Christ and his apostles ... Let them enforce as moral duties ... the great principles of justice and mercy, and all the specific commands and precepts of the Scriptures ... If it be asked what would be the consequence of thus acting on the principles of the gospel, of following the example and obeying the precepts of Christ? We answer, the gradual elevation of the slaves in intelligence, virtue, and wealth; the peaceable and speedy extinction of slavery ... It may be objected that if the slaves are allowed so to improve as to become freemen, the next step in their progress is that they should become citizens. We admit that it is so.*

Like most of his Old School brethren, Hodge held to a gradualist position on emancipation, equally deploring both abolitionist 'immediatism', that slaveholding was a sin and must cease at once, and the pro-slavery position that had gained traction among Southern clergy during the 1840s and 1850s. He believed that if the principles of the gospel prevailed in society, slavery would eventually come to a peaceful end; but liberating the slaves before they were ready for freedom would be irresponsible. Hodge was a product of his age, caught in the web of this all-consuming social dilemma, and like so many nineteenth-century Christians he could not differentiate plainly between race-based black American slavery and color-blind biblical slavery. Africans had been cruelly kidnapped and shipped to America, and there would be no justice for the victims of this heinous crime until much blood had been spilt.

# Seminary life

In addition to the ongoing national crisis over slavery in the States, there was a growing anxiety over the rising numbers of Roman Catholics immigrating to the United States. Most Americans perceived their nation as Protestant, and many viewed Catholicism as a threat to both Protestantism and political liberty. Three million European immigrants made their way to America in the 1840s and 1850s, and the vast majority of them were Roman Catholics from Germany or Ireland. By the time of the Civil War, Catholics would be the largest denomination in America. There was organized political animosity towards Catholics. For example, the 'Know-Nothings' party, which was pledged to protect America from foreigners and Catholics, sent seventy-five men to Congress in 1854. Unfortunately, anti-Catholic sentiment also made its way into ecclesiastical policy.

In 1845, the Presbyterian General Assembly voted overwhelmingly to require the rebaptism of Roman Catholics who desired to become members of the Presbyterian Church. This was a reversal of its historic practice, and Charles Hodge chastised his brethren for this departure from tradition in his annual overview of the General Assembly in the *Biblical Repertory*. Hodge decried this action as a novelty, unknown in other Protestant bodies and opposed to the practice of Protestant bodies ever since the time of the Reformation. Are we to suggest that Luther, Calvin, and untold thousands of other Protestants who only had 'Romish baptism' (no rebaptism) were actually unbaptized persons? What new light has been shed on this question to overturn the custom of the Protestant reformers?

In rebuttal of the Assembly's action, Hodge proceeded to offer his reasons for dissenting from this innovation. He argued that this question had been settled since the ancient church, when church leaders determined that rebaptism was only appropriate when a previous baptism was not Trinitarian. There were heretical groups in the early church which denied the doctrine of the Trinity, and practiced baptism; and there were other sectarian groups which, though Trinitarian in belief, had separated from the church over other disagreements. The Council of Nicaea, for example, made a clear distinction between the necessity of rebaptism of heretics who denied the Trinity and sectarians who differed on lesser issues. The point at issue, argued Hodge, was whether or not a person's baptism was genuinely Trinitarian: this was where the line should be drawn. According to Hodge, there was not a church on earth which affirmed the doctrine of the Trinity 'more accurately, thoroughly or minutely' than the Church of Rome. He boldly demurred that there was no such thing as Trinitarian baptism anywhere if Roman Catholic baptism was not considered Christian baptism.

Hodge offered a definition of legitimate Christian baptism under a three-fold test. Was the baptism in the name of the Trinity, performed with water and with the proper intention? Obviously, Catholics invoked the name of the Trinity in the act of baptism and utilized water. The proper intention had to do with the baptized persons being formally constituted as members of the visible church and being partakers of its blessings. This third test was shared by both the Protestant and Roman Catholic practice of baptism.

The difference between Protestant and Catholic baptism had to do with understanding the immediate efficacy of the sacrament. For Romanists, the baptism of the infant actually conveyed the benefits that were signified in the rite. Protestants differed among themselves on this issue; some (Lutherans, Anglicans) believed, like Catholics, that the child or adult baptized received the Holy Spirit through the act of baptism itself, i.e., baptismal regeneration. Other Protestants viewed baptism as an outward sign only. Still others believed that grace was conveyed in the sacrament, though not limited to the time of administration. If some objected that baptism was null and void if administered by those who believed in the doctrine of baptismal regeneration, then, said Hodge, 'We shall have to unchurch almost the whole Christian world.' He included in the list of those affirming baptismal regeneration not only Catholics, Anglicans, and Lutherans, but also the 'churches of the East' — the Eastern Orthodox family of churches. Hodge concluded his argument by stating that in the Assembly's action to declare Roman Catholic baptism invalid, Presbyterians who have historically been 'catholic' would become 'one of the narrowest and most bigoted of sects'.

Hodge took heat over his comments in the *Biblical Repertory* on Roman Catholic baptism. He replied to his critics in a follow-up article the next year, 'Is the Church of Rome Part of the Visible Church?' Here Hodge declared that Roman Catholics profess 'the essentials of the true Christian religion' despite corruption and abuses. Catholics affirmed the ecumenical creeds and so should be considered part of the visible church. One observes in the baptism controversy the magnanimous spirit of Charles Hodge, who would not countenance excluding Rome as part of the church catholic regardless of ecclesiastical pressure and the anti-Catholic culture of the era.

# 5

# THE CHURCH QUESTION

When Dr Samuel Miller's health declined in the mid-1840s, Hodge took on Miller's seminary lectures on church polity. A number of these lectures were turned into articles published in the *Biblical Repertory*, where he addressed questions related to various theories of church government and debated fine points of Presbyterian practice. Protestants had never agreed on the 'biblical' understanding of church government; whether it be Congregational, Episcopal, or Presbyterian in structure. Some Episcopalians argued that only a church with bishops was the true form of the church, while certain strict Presbyterians had likewise declared that only the system of elders and church courts was legitimately biblical. Hodge would debate both Episcopalians and his fellow Presbyterians as he articulated his understanding of a more biblical and historically Protestant view of the church.

The 'church question' was a significant international theological discussion among scholars of the mid-nineteenth century. It took a variety of forms in Protestant circles as the different bodies revisited their own doctrines of the church and distinctive ecclesiastical practices. In Britain these questions were asked anew by the Oxford Movement, also known as Puseyism or 'Tractarianism', which derived its name from *Tracts for the Times* written by several Anglican theologians including E. B. Pusey, John Henry Newman, and John Keble. Tractarianism was concerned with worldliness and doctrinal laxity within the Church of England, calling for a return to the values of dogma, holiness, apostolic succession, and catholicity. Openness to Roman Catholic perspectives came to characterize the movement, and some of its leaders in time converted to Catholicism.

The *Tracts* created quite a stir in Great Britain, and numerous books were published in order to counter the Oxford Movement. Hodge noted five of these books in an 1842 article, 'The Rule of Faith', so titled because the heart of the matter was whether authority was due to tradition or Scripture as 'the only infallible rule of faith and practice'. Romanists, said Hodge, are doubling their efforts to spread their errors, and now they have found assistance in the *Oxford Tracts*. The Oxford men were arguing from tradition for the very points which separate Protestants and Catholics, such as baptismal regeneration, the real presence, and apostolic succession. The bulk of Hodge's article rehearsed the historical untrustworthiness of church councils, church fathers, and creeds, which have all contradicted one another. There was no consensus in tradition except on the very basic doctrines of the faith concerning Christ. Therefore, any claim that the church has always believed distinctive Roman doctrines was patently false. He concluded, 'The Bible alone

# The church question

is the religion of Protestants ... A better, surer rule than inspired Scripture we cannot have; and it must stand alone, or fall.'

In America, concern for 'the church question' was voiced from a small German Reformed seminary in Mercersburg, Pennsylvania. Several professors at the school began to publish works that questioned the revivalist individualism permeating American Protestantism, calling for a fresh commitment to the corporate life of the church based upon the Reformation heritage with its high view of ecclesiology. This became known as 'Mercersburg theology'. Mercersburg men were concerned about the sectarianism that this neglect of church history had produced. Chief architects of the new Mercersburg movement were John W. Nevin and Philip Schaff. John Nevin had been the Princeton graduate who taught Hodge's Bible courses at the seminary when he studied in Europe during the 1820s. Nevin served as professor of theology at the Presbyterian Western Theological Seminary for ten years and then moved to Mercersburg in 1840. Philip Schaff was a Swiss church historian at the German Reformed Seminary, known for his multi-volume *History of Christianity*, *Creeds of Christendom*, and editing the English translations of the Nicene and Post-Nicene Fathers. Both men called for a return to historic tradition as the remedy for what ailed American Christianity.

The first foray upon Christian individualism was Nevin's 1843 book, *The Anxious Bench*, which attacked the disorderly 'system of the bench' which produced a faith dependent on feeling rather than one nurtured in the church. Nevin addressed sectarianism in a sermon on

'Catholic Unity' before a joint Convention of the Reformed Dutch and German Reformed churches, calling for the visible unity of the catholic (universal) church. Schaff picked up this theme in his inaugural lecture at Mercersburg, which he subsequently expanded into the book, *The Principle of Protestantism*, published in 1845. Schaff advocated an 'evangelical Catholicism', as opposed to what he observed in American Protestantism, which uncritically accepted sectarianism, neglecting the Reformation theology of the church and sacraments. He disclaimed 'Romanism' in the book, but in Protestant America much of this sounded too Roman Catholic. Nevin and Schaff were both accused of 'Romanizing tendencies' even within the German Reformed Synod, but they were never convicted of heresy.

Hodge reviewed Schaff's *The Principle of Protestantism* in the pages of the *Biblical Repertory*, agreeing with Schaff on the essential Protestant principles of justification by faith and Scripture; but he took issue with the charge of sectarianism. For Hodge, the unique American denominational context had actually fostered Christian brotherhood. External unity itself was no sign of genuine unity. In fact, European state churches, while outwardly united, were in actuality more divided among themselves than American churches. He also argued that ecclesiastical separation may be a Christian's duty when unscriptural terms of communion were involved.

The next year, Nevin addressed the Reformation view of the sacraments in his book, *The Mystical Presence, A Vindication of the Reformed or Calvinistic Doctrine of the Holy Eucharist*. Hodge delayed responding to this work for a couple of years, but finally offered a rebuttal in 1848, accusing Nevin of departure from the Reformed tradition. In the book Nevin had argued for the 'real spiritual presence' of Christ in the Lord's Supper against the 'modern Puritans' of American Calvinism, who taught a mere memorial understanding. Hodge wrote that Nevin had distorted the meaning of the Lord's Supper in his emphasis on the believer's union with the divine and human natures of Christ in communion. Nevin and Hodge fundamentally disagreed in their interpretation of John Calvin's teaching on the nature of Christ's presence in the Lord's Supper.

One aspect of the 'church question' had to do with episcopal ordination as an expression of apostolic succession. The first tract (1833) of the Oxford Movement was anonymously written in support of apostolic succession by John Henry Newman, who would become a Roman Catholic in 1845. The Oxford Movement was reacting to liberalism within the Church of England, and the remedy was returning to a 'high church' Anglicanism with renewed attention to the ancient and medieval church rather than the Reformation. Returning to antiquity as an answer meant that the doctrine of 'apostolic succession', typically identified with Roman Catholicism, garnered much attention. There was significant dissent to this 'Romanizing' influence both within the English Church and by American Episcopalians. Hodge published reviews of this dissent in the *Biblical Repertory*, pointing to where Presbyterians agreed with the 'low church' party among the Episcopalians.

For the April 1854 issue of the *Biblical Repertory*, Hodge wrote 'The Church of England and Presbyterian Orders', in which he argued that the key founders and theologians of Anglicanism had not considered episcopacy essential to the being of the church. The recent problem had been caused by the 'Romanizing party' (Tractarians) in the Church of England. Making episcopal ordination essential to both Christian ministry and the efficacy of the sacraments was anti-Protestant and exclusive, making its adherents guilty of sinful schism. Protestant principles required profession of the true religion as the essential element of an organized group being recognized by other Christians as a part of the church catholic. External episcopal organization was not the *sine qua non* of the true ministry and church.

Notwithstanding Hodge's benevolent attitude toward other Christian denominations, he believed that general principles of church government were provided in Scripture *jure divino* (binding upon Christians). Within these principles, the church was free to listen to the Spirit's wisdom as to the most effective functioning of the church in changing times and places. Summarizing his views in 1855, Hodge listed the general principles he saw in the Bible:

1. The right of the people to take part in the government of the church. Hence the divine right of the office of ruling elders, who appear in all church courts as representatives of the people;
2. The appointment and perpetual continuance of Presbyters as ministers of the Word and sacraments, with authority to rule, teach and ordain, as the highest permanent officers of the Church;
3. The unity of the church, or the subjection of a smaller to a larger part, and of a larger part to the whole.

Professor Hodge was a Presbyterian by conviction. Therefore, he argued for Presbyterianism as the biblical form of government; but this did not preclude him from acknowledging other organized Christian bodies as true churches with true ministers. For Hodge, the true church consisted of all those chosen for salvation, which included the saints in heaven and upon earth. Thus it was not to be solely identified with any visible, earthly organization. This 'true spiritual church' was connected to the visible church on earth, and its members are identified among one another by a credible confession of Christ and a corresponding Christian life. These spiritual members of the church were expected to organize themselves on the earth, but no particular organization may claim divine authority only for their practice of church government as essential for salvation or the being of the church.

The Presbyterian Historical Society of Philadelphia invited Hodge to address them in May 1855. His lecture, 'What is Presbyterianism?', described the essential tenets of the Presbyterian form of government. The address was published by the Presbyterian Board of Education and set in motion a series of interactions with Episcopalians who differed with his perspective. For many Episcopalians the central issue was permanency of the apostolic office, a notion rejected by Presbyterian Hodge. In the midst of the interchange of published articles, his friend, Bishop Charles McIlvaine of Ohio, entered the debate. The ever-polite Hodge wrote to his friend, 'I have made the attempt to examine your argument, and have endeavored to treat you as a friend and advocate of evangelical truth, while I treated your argument as a Presbyterian ... I feel nothing but affection and respect towards you. Indeed I cannot but hope you will regard my review as I do, a mere act of self defense.'

Bishop McIlvaine wrote back to Hodge thanking him for the 'kind and affectionate' letter, stating that he knew his friend would 'aim only at the truth and not at me'. McIlvaine claimed to hold the 'low church' doctrine which was predominant in his church. Apostolic succession referred to the power of ordination, which he understood was also the Presbyterian view. In other words, only 'a certain part of the authority committed to the Apostles was intended to continue in the ministry to the end of the world'. This understanding of apostolic succession was vastly different from 'Romanism and Puseyism', which made the being of the church and the sacrament's saving grace dependent on duly-ordained bishops. For McIlvaine, churches without bishops were 'real churches', though he was certain that Episcopal ordination was essential to the 'full order and model of the primitive church'.

Episcopal and Presbyterian differences were also evident in worship. In July 1855, Dr Hodge addressed the issue of Christian worship in an article entitled, 'Presbyterian Liturgies'. The article was a review of *Eutaxia, or the Presbyterian Liturgies: Historical Sketches by a Minister of the Presbyterian Church.* The author was Charles W. Baird, who had the unique experience of spending many years in Europe being exposed to the rich Reformed liturgical heritage. The name *Eutaxia* came from the Greek words translated 'decently and in order' in 1 Corinthians 14:40. Baird's book offered an alternative to disorderly frontier revivalist worship by advocating that American Presbyterians return to the practices of historic Reformed worship. Baird's collection of classical Protestant sixteenth- and seventeenth-century liturgies was impressive in its historical research and drew extensive attention in the church.

In his review of Baird's work, Hodge concurred with the call for liturgical reform, asserting that the use of a set liturgy was not only the domain of Episcopalians, but indeed all Protestants of the Reformation era had adopted their own liturgies, including Presbyterians. He acknowledged that abandonment of these worship patterns by many Protestants had been detrimental to the life of the church. While he agreed with Presbyterians' historic resistance to imposing the Anglican *Book of Common Prayer*, he thought providing optional liturgies for the sacraments, ordination, marriage, and burial could be useful to Presbyterian congregations.

In addition to his mid-century preoccupation with church questions, Hodge also engaged the critical questions related to biblical authority that were emerging in both Europe and America. Hodge wrote several articles touching on the nature of religious language, interacting with the thought of Congregational minister Horace Bushnell and Professor Edward Amasa Park of Andover Seminary. Bushnell had presented lectures to the students at Harvard, Yale, and Andover which were collected in the book, *God in Christ* (1849). The book included a 'Dissertation on Language' as a preface which argued that the nature of abstract religious language was poetical, not literal. Bushnell claimed that theological statements would always be imprecise, because spiritual realities cannot be expressed adequately in human language. Hodge perceived this proposal as a dangerous subjectivism, making doctrinal propositions unimportant in religion. For Hodge, Christianity contained rational doctrinal truths that could be expressed in language; without this there would be no cognitive content to the faith.

The next year Hodge addressed the topic of religious language again in a review of 'The Theology of the Intellect and that of the Feelings', an address by Professor Park to a gathering of Congregational ministers in Boston. The address was Park's attempt to find a middle way between Bushnell's emphasis on subjective feelings and intellectual theology. According to Park, some figurative religious language expressed the feelings and should not be taken literally, but theologians could translate this language into doctrine for the intellect. The theologies of intellect and feeling therefore expressed the truth in different ways. Hodge responded that even figurative language should have definite meaning which satisfies the intellect. There are not two distinct theologies of intellect and emotion, but they are harmoniously joined in Christian experience as Scripture teaches.

After Hodge's initial criticism of Park's sermon, a rejoinder was published by Park to which Hodge replied again in a lengthy 1851 article. Park's thesis was that emotive theology and rational theology can be one in substance though expressed in a different way. The conflicting creeds of men could be harmonized if one understood the difference between poetry (feeling) and prose (propositions), which would clear up misunderstandings between diverse theological perspectives. Hodge replied that claiming that contradictory systems of theology were mere 'logomachy' (dispute about words) cannot pass the test of history. He

# The church question

provided a list of historical disputes over the doctrines of original sin, regeneration, and the atonement which were much more than a misunderstanding over words. Irreconcilable systems of doctrine cannot be explained away by appeals to shared religious sentiment.

Park had written that the theology of reason may become antiquated by the progress of science, but the theology of the heart may hold to the old statements even if they were incorrect. For Hodge, this meant that right feeling may express itself in wrong intellectual forms: therefore, no one Christian theology was exclusively true or timeless. If the biblical writers were understood as presenting truth only within the limitations of their own education and modes of thought, then progressive theology of a later age might improve it. Hodge argued that Park's theory was opposed to what the Bible taught about the importance of truth as revealed by divine revelation in logical propositions addressed to the understanding.

Hodge directly addressed the question of biblical authority in a comprehensive October 1857 article, *The Inspiration of Scripture, its Nature and Proof.* He wrote, 'Faith in Christ, therefore, of necessity involves faith in the Scriptures, and faith in the Scriptures involves the belief that they are the word of God and not the word of man.' And this position was consistent, said Hodge, with an admission that there may be many intellectual difficulties associated with this view. It was important to solve these difficulties, but 'our faith is in no degree dependent on the success of these endeavors'. Stating that 'the Bible is the word of God' meant that 'Everything which the Bible affirms to be true is true.' It was truth based not on the authority of Moses, the prophets, or apostles, but on God's authority.

This understanding of Scripture, according to Hodge, was the doctrine of the whole Christian Church. This had been the historic position of the Greek Church, Catholicism, and Protestants. Hodge asserted, 'All Christians in every age and of every name have regarded the Bible in all its parts as in such a sense the word of God as to be infallible and of divine authority.' This 'church doctrine' was opposed to any notion that only some parts of the Bible are inspired, or that only the moral and religious truths in the Bible are inspired but not historical or geographical details.

Inspiration extended to the very words of the Bible and not merely to thoughts. The supernatural control of the Holy Spirit over the minds of the biblical writers of necessity included the very language they used. If the end was communication of the truth, and communication is in human language, then it must be the case that the Spirit determined the language to communicate the truth in the Scripture. Hodge illustrated this point by the recorded discourses of the Lord. The infallible correctness of the apostolic report of these discourses 'involves the propriety and fitness of the language used to convey the thoughts to be communicated.' He added, 'To deny, in such cases, the control of the Spirit over the words of the sacred writer, is to deny inspiration altogether.' Another example was the many instances where a New Testament writer appealed to a single Old Testament word or expression to make an argument.

Hodge acknowledged that claiming infallibility had difficulties, but what great doctrine was free from difficulty?

The difficulties are 'miraculously small' when one considered that the Bible contained sixty-six distinct productions with multiple subjects and genres, written by forty different men over a fifteen-hundred-year period. The Bible was written before the birth of science, yet the apparent conflict between science and the Bible had not proven to be a reality. He illustrated this with astronomy's discovery of the mechanism of the universe that brought 'great triumph among infidels and great alarm among believers'; yet the Bible was found to harmonize with these discoveries. Geology had made new claims, but 'Geology will soon be found side by side with astronomy in obsequiously bearing up the queenly train of God's majestic word.'

The most serious difficulties for an advocate of biblical inspiration arose from 'the real or apparent inconsistencies, contradictions, and inaccuracies of the sacred volume'. These inconsistencies are 'wonderfully few and trivial' and do not concern matters of doctrine and duty but 'numbers, dates, and historical details'. Some of the inconsistencies may be reconciled; others may not because of ignorance. Hodge explained, 'There are so many errors of transcription in the text of Scripture, such obscurity as to matters necessary to elucidate these ancient records, so little is known of contemporary history, that a man's faith in the divinity of the Bible must be small indeed, if it be shaken because he cannot harmonize the conflicting dates and numbers in Kings and Chronicles.'

All the objections to infallible inspiration were superficial, for the real ground of dissent was deeper. The primary reason that the historic church doctrine of Scripture was being rejected had to do with its incongruence with the 'reigning philosophy' of Germany concerning the nature of God and religion. Hodge pointed to Schleiermacher and other German theologians who had reinterpreted Christianity as a form of religious feeling or consciousness, making the New Testament merely a record of the scenes which awakened the religious consciousness of the apostles. Nothing but human authority can be attributed to the Bible, and men 'receive just what pleases them and reject what they dislike, or what conflicts with their critical or philosophical principles'. Some holding the modern theory taught that there was no distinction between some religions as true and others as false. But, said Hodge, 'Nothing can be more opposed to Scripture than this depreciation of the importance of doctrine ... truth is as essential to holiness as light is to vision.' How can this merely human Bible agree with 'Thus said the Lord', which was found throughout the Scriptures? Hodge demurred, 'It is lamentable when open infidels take this ground; but it is enough to make a man cover his face with his hands in shame, to see those who profess to be Christians, and who are set for the defense of the gospel, through treachery, vanity, or weakness, assuming the same position.'

In the same year that Hodge masterfully addressed the doctrine of Scripture, he also wrote a significant theological defense of Augustinian theology in the lengthy article, 'Free Agency'. From Hodge's perspective, this issue was central to all theological debates on original sin and efficacious grace. He recognized the complex nature of the topic and the ambiguous terminology often used, but every system of theology must speak to this question. As was his custom in writing, he broke the topic down concisely into its various components and moved step-by-step through the very challenging subject, demonstrating an impressive grasp of historic debate which had set the parameters of the discussion.

Hodge wrote that all theories of the will may be classed under three categories. The first category, 'necessity', is the doctrine of fatalism, which precluded all liberty of human action, since all events are determined by a blind necessity. One version of this theory made God the only agent, thereby removing all responsibility from man. A second category of theories he described under the designation 'contingency'. This view, sometimes called the 'power of contrary choice', asserted that the will was independent of reason, feeling, or God and was completely self-determining. Its advocates believed that 'contingency' was essential to liberty of the will; thus there was no certainty of future events. The third theory he classed under the rubric of 'certainty', which was not the same as 'necessity', though the two are often confused.

Hodge offered a lengthy discussion of how 'certainty' did not conflict with human responsibility. Utilizing the framework of St Augustine, Hodge argued that human free agency and the bondage of the will in sin may both be affirmed as true. Liberty and ability are often confused. Man was a free agent (human liberty) determined by nothing outside himself; but a man's ability to will was determined by what was within — his principles, nature, and character. Hodge wrote, 'An agent may be determined with inevitable certainty as to his acts, and yet those acts remain free.' There were numerous ways to illustrate this point from Scripture. God the Father is a free agent, yet it is certain that he will always do what is right. Christ had a complete human soul, but it was certain that he would be without sin. The saints in heaven continue to be free agents, yet their acts will eternally be good. Hodge concluded, 'In every aspect, therefore, in which we can contemplate free agency, whether, in God, in the human nature of Christ, in the redeemed in heaven, or in man here on earth, we find that it is compatible with absolute certainty.'

The foreknowledge of God, foreordination, and divine providence were also doctrines of Scripture consistent with free agency. Hodge poignantly stated,

> *If God cannot effectually control the acts of free agents, there can be no prophecy, no prayer, no thanksgiving, no promises, no security of salvation, no certainty whether in the end God or Satan is to be triumphant, whether heaven or hell is to be the consummation. Give us certainty — the secure conviction that a sparrow cannot fall, nor a sinner move a finger, but as God permits and ordains. We must have either God or Satan to rule. And if God has a providence, he must be able to render the free acts of his creatures certain; and therefore certainty must be consistent with liberty. Was it not certain that Christ should, according to the Scriptures, be by wicked hands crucified and slain, and yet were not his murderers free in all they did?*

Hodge argued in conclusion that his articulation of free agency was the 'faith of the whole Church'. The Greek, Latin, and Protestant churches all confessed the doctrines of original righteousness, original sin, and regeneration by the Holy Spirit, because they believed these doctrines were taught in the Bible. According to Hodge, the core of Augustine's teaching about fallen humanity and the necessity of grace were affirmed in essence by all Christian churches.

Around this same time, the old question of confessional subscription resurfaced in the Old School Church. In 1858, Hodge wrote his most extensive essay on the subscription issue. The occasion for renewed attention to subscription was the recent overture from the United Synod of the South to the Old School Assembly for reunion. The United Synod was a new Southern denomination that had recently separated from the New School Presbyterian Church over threats of church discipline for church members owning slaves. An additional reason for Hodge's essay was something he had recently written in the *Biblical Repertory* which opposed the idea of Presbyterians producing a Bible commentary in accordance with the *Westminster Confession*. Hodge contended that this was a bad idea since Presbyterian clergy did not even agree on all the details of the confession; much less could it be expected for them to agree on the interpretation of every passage of Scripture!

In his critique of the proposed Bible commentary, Hodge had said of the *Westminster Confession*, 'We could not hold together for a week, if we made the adoption of all its propositions a condition of ministerial communion.' This comment drew the ire of his Old School brethren, who publicly criticized Hodge in church papers for advocating a loose view of subscription. Hodge replied to his critics with the article, 'Adoption of the Confession of Faith', asserting that any suggestion of strict subscription at this juncture in history was very dangerous for the unity of the church.

Expecting ministers to affirm 'every proposition' in the confession was an 'impracticable theory' and would bring 'certain and immediate ruin' to the church. Again Hodge explained his position that adopting the 'system of doctrine' (essential Calvinism) of the confession was all that was required. This was the same position he had articulated for thirty years, and the outcry from his Old School detractors was unjustified.

In addition to rigidity on subscription, some conservative Old School Presbyterians were just as inflexible in their understanding of Presbyterian government. Hodge took a broader view of Presbyterianism and was drawn into debate over church polity at the 1860 General Assembly. For Hodge, who fully embraced church rule by elders as biblical, there was a significant amount of flexibility in church ministry. There are certain prescribed principles of government but beyond these 'there is a wide discretion allowed us by God, in matters of detail'. Hodge's 1855 piece, 'What is Presbyterianism?', had sparked some of the initial discussion leading up to the Assembly debate. The debate would be followed by articles in several periodicals, including 'Presbyterianism', written by Hodge for the *Biblical Repertory*.

Hodge's chief opponent at the 1860 Assembly debate was the eloquent James Henley Thornwell of South Carolina. Thornwell served as professor of theology at Columbia Theological Seminary and as supply pastor of the First Presbyterian Church. Dr Thornwell argued that the Bible provided more than mere general principles of polity, and any ecclesiastical action without specific warrant from the Word of God was unlawful. The primary point in the debate concerned the legitimacy of church boards, which Hodge defended as consistent with Presbyterianism. Thornwell wanted to jettison church boards and replace them with committees more directly tied to the church courts. Opposition was voiced to the Board of Missions as unscriptural. Hodge countered that committees were likewise a delegated body; thus there was no real difference between the two. After Thornwell's impassioned speech, Hodge gave a forty-minute rebuttal, convincing the Assembly, which overwhelmingly voted to keep the church boards.

The heart of the debate over church government related to a diversity of opinion on interpreting the old 'regulative principle' of the seventeenth-century English Presbyterian Puritans. This principle essentially stated that anything not explicitly commanded in Scripture was forbidden to the church. Thornwell interpreted the principle as opposed to churchly liberty of discretion, but Hodge countered that this was a misunderstanding. In fact, the Puritans were resisting the very thing Thornwell was attempting to foist upon the church — taking an individual inference drawn from Scripture and attempting to make this mandatory for the conscience of the whole church. Hodge accused Thornwell of 'high churchism' and impeding the church's great operations by 'abstractions'. These views were impractical, and logic would demand that the church disband the boards of her colleges and seminaries too.

Another issue that surfaced in the Assembly debate was the relationship between ministers and ruling elders. Thornwell argued that elders and ministers are one order/office in the church, while Hodge advocated a clear distinction between clergy and lay elders. For Hodge, clergy have distinct gifts, training, ordination, and duties in church life, whereas lay elders have unique roles as chosen representatives of the congregation. Elders rule in the church through the exercise of government and discipline; professional ministers, conversely, have a special calling to preach and administer the sacraments. Hodge believed that his position safeguarded lay leadership in the local church and represented the views of historic Presbyterianism. After his death, A. A. Hodge collected his father's many articles on church government issues into a single volume, *The Church and its Polity*, published in 1879.

Hodge encountered another famous Southern theologian in 1860. Princeton was seeking to fill the chair of ecclesiastical history and ecclesiology and looked favorably towards the respected Dr Robert Lewis Dabney of Virginia. Professor Dabney was teaching theology at Union Seminary and serving the College Church at Hampton-Sydney. Hodge wrote to Dabney three times imploring him to move to Princeton and assist them in the labors of the seminary. Dabney candidly declined, because it would cause him 'to rupture the ties of affection and dependence which bind me to my servants ... and subject my wife to domestic arrangements untried by her'. His letter concealed the obvious reason he could not come to Princeton — war was on the horizon, and he would be forced to return home to the South. Within the next two years Dabney would be serving the Confederacy as chaplain to General Thomas 'Stonewall' Jackson.

# 6

# WAR AND REUNION

Increasing fears about the 'irrepressible conflict' descended upon American churches, causing denominational division across the country during the 1850s. New School Presbyterian Assemblies had been frequently troubled by the slavery question, unlike the Old School, which had an unspoken agreement that slavery would not be discussed publicly. In 1853, the New School Assembly asked all presbyteries to give a progress report on rooting out the evils of slavery; the request was ignored by Southern New School Presbyterians. By 1856, New School abolitionists urged disciplinary action, and Southerners, believing that their liberty of conscience was being violated, finally departed to form a southern New School church. The United Synod of the South, which was organized in Knoxville in 1858, vowed that 'political agitation' and 'ultra abolitionist sentiments' would have no part in their denomination. The United Synod immediately made overtures to the Old School body for reunion discussions, but the Old School church was not interested in 1858. This attitude would alter noticeably as the War Between the States progressed.

When the Civil War began in 1861, the New School (North) was firmly with the Union, having already purged itself of the Southern contingent. The case was very different in the Old School, which had been able to maintain ecclesiastical unity despite sectional pressures. The Old School Presbyterian Church managed to sustain ecclesiastical oneness by taking a more conservative stance on slavery than that pursued by the New School. Typical of the Old School attitude were two resolutions adopted by the 1845 General Assembly: 'Resolved, 1st That the General Assembly of the Presbyterian Church in the United States was originally organized, and has since continued the bond of union in the Church upon the conceded principle that the existence of domestic slavery, under the circumstances in which it is found in the southern portion of this country is no bar to Christian communion.' The second resolution declared that to raise the question of church discipline for the holding of slaves was to be deplored 'as tending to the dissolution of the union of our beloved country, and which every enlightened Christian will oppose as bringing about a ruinous and unnecessary schism between brethren who maintain a common faith'. As long as this attitude prevailed, peace in the Old School body was secure.

One of the primary arguments for keeping the abolitionist cause out of ecclesiastical deliberations was the doctrine of the 'spirituality of the church'. Slavery was a civil relation and therefore belonged to the political sphere. The church can only say what the Bible says, no more and no less, and the Bible does not declare slavery sinful. Dr Thornwell of South Carolina forcefully articulated these ideas in his 1851 essay, 'The Relation of the Church to Slavery', which was widely distributed among Southern Presbyterians. For Thornwell, the church should not make public declarations about political questions, but only address itself to spiritual matters. Hodge took issue with this viewpoint, arguing in an 1860 essay that the church could appropriately speak out against social evil if guided to that conclusion by God's Word. As Hodge would later point out, the Southern men were inconsistent with their own principles, because they publicly endorsed slavery and supported the Confederacy. The 1860 General Assembly tried to maneuver a middle course on the 'spirituality of the church', declaring that they had no right to interfere in politics but affirming the right to bear testimony against sin.

With the election in 1860 of Abraham Lincoln, a man whom the South considered a radical on the slavery question, the dissolution of the union appeared imminent. Hodge wrote 'The State of the Country' in early 1861, arguing that the complaints of the South did not justify the dissolution of the Union. The article was written before South Carolina's secession in December 1860, but was not actually published in the *Biblical Repertory* until January 1861. This essay drew more national attention than anything ever written by Hodge. It was reprinted, put in pamphlet form, and disseminated throughout the country. Many hailed it as fair and reasonable, but the South condemned it, as did radical abolitionists in the North.

Hodge had hoped that the Old School Presbyterian Church could remain united even in the midst of national turmoil. He wrote 'The Church and Country' in April 1861 in order to plead his case. In the midst of a divided nation, could not the Presbyterian Church provide a model of Christian brotherhood by maintaining ecclesiastical union? One of the chief obstacles to this unity was a new 'anti-Christian sentiment' among some Southern clergymen, who were now advocating that slavery was something good and to be perpetuated. Hodge's appeal for unity was unheeded and Presbyterians soon divided just like the other Protestant bodies that had already experienced schism.

As hard as the peacemakers tried, they could not stem the rising tide of sectional division that was engulfing America. During the early morning of 12 April 1861, South Carolinians opened fire on Fort Sumter from shore batteries in Charleston. The war had begun. The Old School Assembly convened the next month in Philadelphia with very few Southern commissioners in attendance. An amicable spirit prevailed among the brethren, but the inevitable question had to emerge. After twelve days and much debate the moment of truth finally arrived when Dr Gardiner Spring's resolution, affirming loyalty to the federal government, was approved 156 to 66. Immediately a protest was entered by Charles Hodge and fifty-seven other commissioners. The protest declared, 'The General Assembly in thus deciding a political question, and in making that decision practically a condition of membership in the Church, has, in our judgment, violated the Constitution of the Church, and usurped the prerogative of its Divine Master.' The substance of Hodge's dissent was that a church court had no right to demand that it was the duty of citizens in the seceding states to support the federal government. While Christians are taught to support the powers that be, 'The Bible does not enable any man to decide whether these United States are a nation, or a voluntary confederacy of nations, the church has no voice in the decision of this question.'

The protest was rebuffed and Southern Presbyterians, asserting that they had been unconstitutionally debarred by the Assembly, began to withdraw in order to form a new and independent church. Southern indignation was expressed by each synod as it formally withdrew from the Old School Assembly over the next few months. To have remained a part of the Northern Assembly would have been tantamount to treason in the Southern mind. The Presbyterian Church in the Confederate States of America was established in 1861 by Southern presbyteries assembled at First Presbyterian Church in Augusta, Georgia. The pastor of First Presbyterian was Dr Joseph Wilson, father of Thomas Woodrow Wilson, twenty-eighth president of the United States. By 1861, there were four Presbyterian bodies in the United States — an Old School and New School church in both the North and South. Southerners would be the first to reunite; the Old School and New School Southern churches officially reunited in 1864.

Dr Hodge was loyal to the Union throughout the War Between the States, believing that 'God is on our side'. He voiced his dismay at England's siding with the South, since obviously all Southern grievances were directed at the interests of slavery. Writing in 1862, Hodge was indignant: 'That English anti-slavery Christians should sustain a rebellion made to conserve, perpetuate, and extend slavery, was a moral phenomenon that astonished the Christian world.' In 1863, with the Civil War dragging on, he inserted himself into political discussions again by appealing for support of the war effort and the president. By this time there was significant opposition to Lincoln's prosecution of the war, resentment of suspending the writ of *habeas corpus*, and questions about his authority to issue the Emancipation Proclamation. Hodge supported the president's positions as legitimate during a time of war. At the end of the war, he wrote, 'The first and most obvious consequence of the dreadful civil war just ended, has been the final and universal overthrow of slavery within the limits of the United States. This is one of the most momentous events in the history of the world. That it was the design of God to bring about this event cannot be doubted.'

When President Lincoln was murdered on 14 April 1865, Charles Hodge was overcome with emotion. As faculty and students met on campus for prayer, one student recalled how he had never forgotten that day and hearing his professor sobbing as he led the students in prayer. In the next issue of the *Biblical Repertory*, Hodge penned an article on President Lincoln describing the nation as a widow. He wrote, 'It was not merely sorrow for the loss of a great man when most needed, or of one who had rendered his country inestimable service, but grief for a man whom every one personally loved.' He also appealed to the nation to emulate Lincoln's compassion towards the South.

While he was a Union man, after the cessation of hostilities, Hodge disagreed with the government's oppressive reconstruction policies imposed upon the South. He also differed with his denomination's 'extreme measures of ecclesiastical reconstruction' driven by anger after the assassination of Lincoln. The Presbyterian General Assembly, meeting in Pittsburgh a month after Lincoln's death, issued what came to be known as the 'Pittsburgh orders', labeling secession a sin for which Southerners must repent before readmission to the Presbyterian Church. Hodge criticized the Assembly for its position because secession was not an ecclesiastical sin; in fact, 'All admit, revolution and rebellion are right on certain occasions, and no church has the right to decide upon those conditions.' He also pointed out a serious flaw in this unjust policy, because 'thousands of people at the North sympathized with the South, and in many ways gave aid and comfort to the rebels'. No one was calling for these Northerners to repent. The 'Pittsburgh orders' were never enforced.

Feelings were always intense in the border states of Missouri and Kentucky, both during and after the war. One of Hodge's former students, Dr Samuel M' Pheeters of Raleigh, North Carolina, was dismissed in 1863 from the Pine Street Church by the Presbytery of St Louis on specious grounds. Hodge publicly criticized the 1864 General Assembly for upholding a lower court's removal of M' Pheeters, who was being punished for his feelings about the South. Hodge earnestly protested this injustice indicating that M' Pheeters was a solid minister and citizen, having taken an oath of allegiance to the Union. There was continual harassment of Southern sympathizers in Missouri and Kentucky, which finally drove the Synod of Kentucky to withdraw from the Northern Old School and unite with the Southern Presbyterian Church in 1869. The Synod of Missouri joined the Southern Church in 1874. Hodge took a lot of heat for his conciliatory attitudes towards Southerners and their sympathizers. In one small presbytery, the ministers petitioned the 1866 General Assembly to direct Professor Hodge to desist 'corrupting the minds of the young men in the Seminary, in regard to their church and country.'

At the war's end, Hodge called for union with the Southern Presbyterian brethren, believing that it would honor Christ. The Episcopalians were united and so were the Romanists. Why couldn't Presbyterians become the third national church body? The great need of the hour was to rebuild the nation, and reconciliation between the Northern and Southern churches would contribute to this necessary reconstruction. This was not to be. While the Old School and New School in the North would eventually reunite in 1869, sectional differences ran too deep and the painful memories of the war lingered. There were several attempts in the later decades of the nineteenth century to reunite the two bodies, all to no avail. It would be more than one hundred years (1983) before Presbyterians were able to reconnect the two major portions of the church that had been separated since the Civil War.

Hodge expressed mixed feelings about his Old School church reuniting with the Northern New School Presbyterians. Before any formal reunion discussions between the two Presbyterian branches in the North began, Hodge publicly asked the question, in an article 'On Principles of Church Union' (1865), whether it was the duty of the Old School/New School bodies to unite and become one church. He stated that the union was desirable if it could occur without the 'sacrifice of principle' and if it could be a 'real and harmonious' union. For Hodge, the causes of the 1837 Presbyterian division had centered in a disagreement over the rightful exercise of discipline. He explained, 'As to doctrine, the difference was not that all the Old-school were orthodox and all the New-school heterodox; not that errors which a large part of the New-school party rejected did in fact more or less prevail among our ministers and churches; but the great and vital difference was, whether these errors should be a bar to ministerial communion.'

This diversity over discipline in doctrinal matters stemmed from distinct perspectives on the sense in which subscription to the Confession was to be understood. Discipline and admission to ministerial office in the New School (at least in some quarters) was governed by a perspective that viewed subscription as only binding one to the 'essential and necessary doctrines' of Christianity, not Calvinism *per se*. This interpretation the Old School had implicitly disavowed by its condemnation of errors in 1837. Hodge's conviction was that the New School separated from the Old School; therefore, it was a question of whether or not the New School wanted to return to the Presbyterian Church. Was the New School willing to exercise proper discipline by requiring candidates for ordination and ordained ministers to embrace the Calvinistic system of doctrine, as presented in the *Westminster Confession of Faith*? If they were willing to do this, Hodge could offer no conscientious objection to their return. When reunion discussions officially commenced in 1866, Hodge fully immersed himself in these issues in the pages of the *Biblical Repertory*, and in several instances found himself in the eye of the storm. In his annual published reviews on the General Assembly during the reunion negotiation years (1866–1870), he consistently questioned the New School's authentic commitment to the confession because of the New School's historic practice of 'broad church' principles.

A number of factors paved the way for a climate favorable for union among the former Old School/New School adversaries in the Presbyterian Church. From the beginning of the war, the Northern New School Church was intensely loyal to the Federal Government and abhorred slavery and the Southern rebellion that supported this evil institution. Southerners in both parties had now departed and the Northern Old School had been both loyal to the Federal Government and more critical of slavery as the war years progressed. Even with the removal of these obstacles, when reunion discussions began, both parties perceived the other as rigid and a compromiser of Presbyterian principles. It became clear very early that the question of confessional subscription would be the principal stumbling block along the road to reunion. Meetings of the Joint Committee revealed, however, that there was more accord on this issue than either side realized.

Ultimately, Hodge was not convinced that the New School had altered its course; therefore he became outspokenly opposed to the reunion. In the 1867 *Biblical Repertory* review of the General Assembly, Hodge charged the New School with holding an 'evasive subscription'; thus reunion plans were unacceptable. He accused the New School of harboring 'latitudinarian' subscription, that is, a broad 'substance of doctrine' or 'essentials of Christianity only' view which did not require adoption of the 'system of doctrine' in the Confession as historically understood. Hodge was answered by New School spokesman Henry B. Smith (1815–1877), professor of theology at New York's Union Seminary. Smith countered that the New School rejected the extremes of either latitude or a strict 'every proposition' view. Dr Smith argued for a median position on subscription which called for subscription to the 'Reformed or Calvinistic system' of the Confession of Faith, and he cited favorably Hodge's 1831 article on confessional subscription. Hodge later admitted that Smith's position was the same view he held.

Smith believed that the 'groundless imputations' of doctrinal unsoundness, latitudinarianism, and dishonest subscription attacked the faith and honor of New School men. These accusations had been met with the 'unanimous denial of all our journals'. He resented the tone of Hodge's article, which he said attempted 'to claim a monopoly, not only on Presbyterian orthodoxy, but also of the Presbyterian conscience'. The suggestion that New School men on the Joint Committee had 'hoodwinked' the Old School men, by misrepresenting the 'real views' of the church, was not credible. 'Nobody can believe that the Joint Committee was so blind, weak and silly.' Hodge had asserted that the present Plan for Union 'abandons the principles' on which the Presbyterian Church was founded. According to Smith, this was a gross exaggeration and a cruel accusation. Smith retorted that, as a matter of fact, the very concessions on doctrine and subscription that Hodge supported in his article are 'all for which we really contend'. Smith added, 'We say that we adopt the principle of subscription which he advocates.' Smith was convinced that reunion would strengthen the mission of the church and remove the reproach brought upon 'our common Christianity' by continued strife and separation. No one could question Smith's Reformed orthodoxy, but uncertainty remained in Hodge's mind as to whether Smith's views reflected the perspective of the whole New School church.

In November 1867, Hodge attended the Presbyterian National Union Convention in Philadelphia. The convention was an attempt to bring all the Presbyterian bodies in America together, and each denomination sent delegations. During the meetings New School delegates gave strong affirmation of the Westminster Standards, which seemed to answer most remaining concerns about New School convictions. At the convention, Smith recommended that the confession should be 'received in its proper historical, that is, the Calvinistic or Reformed sense'. Dr Hodge, who was in the room, whispered to a friend that Smith's position met his approval.

A moving event that transpired at the National Union Convention was an unexpected interchange between the Presbyterians and Episcopalians, who were both meeting in Philadelphia at the time. Word came to the Presbyterians that prayer had been offered for them at the meeting of the Protestant Episcopal Evangelical Societies. The Presbyterian convention reciprocated by sending a delegation, headed by Dr Smith, to bring greetings to the Episcopalians, who in turn sent representatives back to the Presbyterian gathering. After gracious words, prayers, and a benediction by the Episcopalians, Dr Hodge was asked to reply on behalf of the Presbyterian churches. Hodge began with personal reflections on boyhood memories with Bishop McIlvaine, who was present, and then he addressed the Episcopalians,

> *Has not your Church and our Church been rocked in the same cradle? Did they not pass through the same Red Sea, receiving the same baptism of the Spirit, and of fire? Have they not uttered from those days of the Reformation to the*

> *present time, the same great testimony for Christ and his Gospel? What difference, sir, is there between your Thirty-Nine Articles, and our Confession of faith, other than the difference between one part and another of the same great Cathedral anthem rising to the skies? Does it not seem to indicate, sir, that these churches are coming together? We stand here, sir, to say to the whole world, that we are one in faith, one in baptism, one in life, and one in our allegiance to your Lord and to our Lord.*

The words uttered that Friday morning in November 1867 reflected the winsome ecumenical spirit of Charles Hodge in its full flower. Some had speculated that Dr Hodge's esteem in the eyes of his brethren had suffered as a result of opposing both retaliation towards the South and reunion with the New School. However, eyewitnesses testified that as the aged professor reached the platform, spontaneous applause erupted throughout the hall and lasted for some time. The editor of a religious newspaper observed, 'It was the ready homage of Christian men to one who had kept the faith, and taught it, and had ever been foremost in its defense, and so had won his way to the highest confidence and respect of the Church.' No doubt this laudatory reception was in part a result of the hall being filled with a number of his former students.

The Presbyterian National Union Convention accomplished much toward hastening the day of Presbyterian reunion. After much give and take, a Joint Committee of Reunion finally proposed a 'Plan of Union' that was presented to the 1868 General Assemblies of the Old School and New School. Both Assemblies adopted the Plan, but a protest was raised on the Old School side about an 'explanatory clause' in one article that appeared to grant too much doctrinal latitude. New School men raised concern about a controversial provision for re-examining ministers; this had been a sticking-point for the New School, fearful that Old School presbyteries might refuse admission of transferring ministers. Taking into consideration these objections, a revised Plan was re-submitted to both 1869 Assemblies meeting in New York City within walking distance of one another. The Old School voted in favor of union with only nine negative votes; the New School vote for union was unanimous.

Hodge steadily opposed reunion during the years of negotiation, because he believed that the New School church, while orthodox as a whole, was too broad in its practice and would ordain men whom the Old School could not in good conscience. Given this tolerant New School spirit, Hodge maintained doubts that the New School element in a reunited church would have the resolve to exercise discipline. In Hodge's review of the 1869 General Assembly, he recognized that reunion was now a fact and called upon the reunited church to devote its energies to 'a success of real inward unity, animating this external organic union, so that the one body may be inspired by one spirit; that it may be cemented and consolidated in a real, great, and glorious advance of truth, unity, and charity; in an immense growth of sound Christian evangelism, true piety, and of Presbyterian doctrine, order, polity, institutions, life, and manners'. The consummate churchman, Hodge would support the reunited church, despite his own reservations.

# 7

# Legacy

Between 1858 and 1868, Charles Hodge wrote thirty-five articles for the *Biblical Repertory*; also during these years he had begun compiling his massive three-volume *Systematic Theology*. No longer having the energy of a young man, in 1865 he confessed his weariness and the burden of editing the *Biblical Repertory and Princeton Review*. He described the journal as his 'ball and chain for forty years', admitting that its discontinuance would be a 'great relief'. At seventy-one, time was taking its toll and he gladly handed over primary editorial duties for the journal to Lyman Atwater in 1868. Hodge had been sole editor for four decades of his life. Since 1822 he had contributed five thousand pages to the journal, including the writing of 142 articles for publication.

In 1870, an Index Volume for the *Biblical Repertory and Princeton Review* was published, which included a 'Retrospect of the History of the Princeton Review' written by Dr Hodge. In these pages he reflected upon over forty years of the journal's existence. According to Hodge, it remained the enduring conviction of the editors that 'the system of the Reformed Church and Augustinians in all ages, is the truth of God revealed for His glory and the salvation of men'. He added that they also believed that 'the Presbyterian Church, its form of government and discipline, was more conformed than any other to the Scriptural model, and the best adapted for preserving the purity and developing the life of the Church'. It was the vindication of these principles that the editors always kept in view. Hodge summarized the core Calvinistic doctrines defended in the *Biblical Repertory* over the years: 'Men are born into the world, since the fall, in a state of sin and condemnation; ... men are dependent on the Holy Spirit for their regeneration; ... due to the sovereign and supernatural interposition of the Spirit one man is converted and not another'. When these essential truths were affirmed, there was no call for church discipline against any minister. On the other hand, when it was taught that 'men since the fall are not born in sin; ... men have plenary ability to avoid all sin ... that in conversion it is man, and not God, who determines who do, and who do not, turn to God, ... vital principles, not of the Reformed faith only, but even of Catholic Christianity, were involved.'

Hodge made no apology for the controversial nature of many *Biblical Repertory* articles, for 'the Bible is the most controversial of books', being a protest against sin and error. The editors always tried to enter controversy with humility and charity, but contended for the true and right as they understood it from the Word of God. He conceded that there had been failures to meet this lofty standard, but they had tried to the best of their ability. The journal had been conservative, with no interest in originality, but defending 'the doctrines of our standards'. He famously noted, 'Whether it be a ground of reproach or of approbation, it is believed to be true that an original idea in theology is not to be found in the pages of the *Biblical Repertory and Princeton Review* from the beginning until now. The phrase "Princeton Theology," therefore, is without distinctive meaning.' As he reflected on his editorial career, it was clear that Charles Hodge had unfailingly maintained his foundational commitments ever since his early years as a seminary professor.

Arguably Hodge's most influential writing in the coming generations would be his two-thousand-page *Systematic Theology* published near the end of his career. Since the 1840s, Hodge had been giving lectures to his students, who meticulously took notes. The tedious classroom note-taking was so overwhelming that eventually, in 1865, a student named Frederick Wines edited a printed version of the lecture notes, entitled *Systematic Theology: A Series of Questions Upon the Lectures Delivered to Students in Princeton Theological Seminary by the Rev. Charles Hodge, D.D. edited by A Member of the Senior Class and Printed for the Use of the Students*. Meanwhile, at the urging of students, in 1864 Professor Hodge had begun working on a massive manuscript of all his lectures that could be published for students and the church. The revision of his notes continued for several years and finally the three-volume *Systematic Theology* was published in 1872.

The *magnum opus* was divided into four sections: theological method, doctrine of God, doctrine of man, and salvation. Under method in theology, Hodge described three different approaches to theology — speculative, mystical, and the inductive method. Under the speculative category, he placed Deism (rationalism), medieval scholasticism, and Transcendentalism, which all attempted to discern truth by the use of human reason and minimized divine revelation. By contrast, the mystical method promoted the use of human feelings as the primary basis of religious truth. There were two versions of this approach to theology, a supernatural and a natural mysticism. The supernatural mystic emphasized finding truth through feelings and intuitions apart from the Bible whereas a naturalistic scheme searched for religious meaning in human consciousness. A chief advocate of the latter view was Friedrich Schleiermacher, who defined religion as a human consciousness of God in his *Christian Faith* (1821–1822). This human feeling of absolute dependence on God has taken a variety of religious forms with the highest expression being Christianity.

Hodge believed speculative and mystic methodologies were inadequate for constructing Christian theology, arguing instead for an inductive method based upon Scripture. He wrote, 'The true method of theology is, therefore, the inductive, which assumes that the Bible contains all the facts or truths which form the contents of theology, just as the facts of nature are the contents of the natural sciences.' Theology was a science, where the data of the Bible were organized and interpreted. There was still a proper subsidiary role for reason and feeling in Hodge's theology, but these sources must always be tested by Scripture. Hodge balanced his objective approach to divine truths revealed in Scripture with a clear affirmation of the essential role of the Holy Spirit in illumining Scripture for the believer. The inner witness of the Spirit illumined the Christian mind to understand the things revealed in the Word.

Hodge's theological method was inseparably connected to his understanding of the Spirit's plenary inspiration of Scripture. Hodge articulated this conviction in the *Systematic Theology*:

> This means, first, that all the books of Scripture are equally inspired. All are alike infallible in what they teach. And secondly, that inspiration extends to all the contents of these several books. It is not confined to moral and religious truths, but extends to the statements of facts, whether scientific, historical, or geographical. It is not confined to those facts the importance of which is obvious, or which are involved in matters of doctrine. It extends to everything which any sacred writer asserts to be true.

Undergirding Hodge's inductive method of biblical study was a philosophical framework that informed how he viewed the world and human beings — a philosophy known as Scottish Common Sense Realism. This philosophy had been developed by Thomas Reid (1710–1796) of Glasgow University, who reasoned that humanity had both an accurate knowledge of the real world and possessed an innate knowledge of basic morality. Scottish philosophy was set in opposition to skepticism, which questioned any certitude. According to Reid, people may gain accurate knowledge of the world by the proper use of the senses. John Witherspoon had introduced Scottish Realism to American students when he began his presidency of the College of New Jersey in 1768. This approach had resonated with

Witherspoon, for he was convinced that Christianity was reasonable and compatible with common sense. Archibald Alexander had likewise taught Common Sense philosophy at Princeton when young Hodge had been a student. In the *Systematic Theology* Hodge operated under these same philosophical assumptions, supposing that these principles should be acceptable to everyone. Scottish Realism shaped American Protestant faith until the middle of the nineteenth century, and Charles Hodge was no exception. Armed with the presuppositions of common sense, the inspiration of Scripture and historic Christian theology, Hodge projected a profound confidence in the theology he championed. Once chided for his certainty, he replied, 'A Christian surrounded by learned skeptics may be deeply sensible of his own weakness, and yet serenely confident in the strength of his cause. We then, who are within those old walls which have stood for ages, even from the beginning, who can look around and see the names of all generations of saints inscribed on those walls, and who feel the solid rock of God's word under their feet, must be excused for a feeling of security.'

The *Systematic Theology* exuded a confidence that the Bible could be understood by God's people as a system of divinely revealed truth. As a clear exposition and ordering of biblical teaching, the three volumes remained popular for a very long time. The *Systematic Theology* would become a primary theological textbook for conservative Presbyterian and Reformed churches in the United States and abroad for the next century. Confessional Reformed theology was evident throughout the volumes, yet Hodge made a point of emphasizing the catholic (universal) faith of the church. This common Christian faith was self-evident in 'the devotional writings of true Christians of every denomination'.

In the same year that Hodge's long-awaited textbook appeared in print, the seminary held a special event celebrating fifty years of Hodge's teaching at Princeton. Over half a century, he had taught 2,700 students; and four hundred of them showed up for the ceremony honoring their professor. In addition to the throng of students, his wife, brother Hugh, children, and grandchildren attended the gathering, along with his colleagues and representatives from various colleges, seminaries, and denominations. The multitude gathered on 24 April 1872 at First Presbyterian Church. They heard numerous addresses (and letters from those unable to attend) extolling the virtues of Dr Hodge's mind and heart, which had blessed the students, seminary community, and church at large.

After listening to the affectionate accolades, the seventy-five-year-old professor was given an opportunity to speak. He told the crowd. 'It is impossible that I should make you understand the feelings which swell my heart almost to bursting ... I can only bow down before you with tearful gratitude, and call on God to bless you, and to reward you a hundredfold for all your goodness.' There was a dinner and reception later at Hodge's home in Princeton. The alumni had raised $45,000 to endow a Charles Hodge chair of systematic theology as well as a $15,000 gift for Dr Hodge. In his journal he described the day as 'the apex of my life', serving as a 'testimony of the unity of the faith and common love to the same gospel'.

The fact that former students venerated Hodge in this way was no surprise, as he had endeared himself to them over many years. In addition to the influence of his teaching and writing on their lives, students remembered with great fondness their beloved professor's warmth and devotion to them as students and ministers. Beginning in 1868, there had been a special graduation tradition at the seminary which displayed this unique bond Hodge had with his former students. At the end of the graduation service, the graduates would gather around Dr Hodge in a circle and sing, 'All Hail the Power of Jesus Name', and then sing together, 'Blest Be the Tie that Binds' and the 'Doxology'. After the songs, the professor would pronounce the benediction and shake hands with each new graduate.

In his twilight years, the old professor received the affectionate accolades due to one who had earned respect over a lifetime. One factor that endeared him to so many was his charitable spirit, which was never as obvious as when he graciously dealt with theological opponents. A steady trait throughout decades of controversy, this spirit was especially evident in his consistent attitude towards Roman Catholics. For example, in his *Systematic Theology*, when commenting on the Catholic view of justification, Hodge confessed, 'Indeed it is a matter of devout thankfulness to God that underneath the numerous grievous and destructive errors of the Romish Church, the great truths of the Gospel are preserved.' When Presbyterians were invited to send observers to the First Vatican Council, Hodge was asked to reply on behalf of the General Assembly. Professor Hodge's 1869 letter to Pope Pius IX described doctrinal reasons why Presbyterians could not attend but then added, 'Although we cannot return to the fellowship of the Church of Rome, we desire to live in charity with all men. We love all those who love our Lord Jesus Christ in sincerity. We regard as Christian brethren all who worship, love, and obey him as their God and Savior.' In May 1872, Hodge was asked his opinion about Roman Catholicism; he answered that 'The Roman Catholic Church teaches truth enough to save the souls of men.' He pointed to Catholic proclamation of the divine authority of Scripture, the obligation of the Ten Commandments, the punishment of eternity, and the call to worship the Trinity. He wrote, '... when the choice is between that [a Roman Catholic church] and none [no church], it is wise and right to encourage the establishment of churches under the control of Catholic priests. For myself, I take this view. The principle cannot be carried out that no church is to be encouraged which teaches error.'

While Hodge's charity extended as far as Catholicism, his solidarity with fellow Protestants ran much deeper. At the fall 1873 meeting of the General Conference of the Evangelical Alliance in New York, Dr Hodge was asked to bring a plenary address to the international group, which had been in existence since 1846. His speech, 'The Unity of the Church based on Personal Union with Christ', emphasized the unity believers shared in Christ and with each other through the indwelling Spirit. Believers scattered over the globe were a band of brothers as children of the same Father. The common religious experience of Christ's followers was a sure basis of Christian fellowship and evidence of the truth of Christianity. While outwardly Protestant groups articulated a diversity of creeds, they shared the same life experiences through conversion, worship, and hymnody.

By virtue of this union in Christ, denominational churches owed three duties to each other: mutual recognition, inter-communion, and recognition of each other's sacraments and order. If Christians really believed these things, said Hodge, churches would cease mutual incriminations and rivalry and instead practice 'mutual respect' and 'cordial co-operation'. This kind of unity would present 'an undivided front against infidelity and every form of Anti-Christian error'. On the question of inter-communion, Hodge asserted, 'No particular church has the right to require any thing as a term of communion which Christ has not made a condition of salvation.' How can denominations refuse to receive those whom Christ has received? Churches cannot alter the conditions of salvation, nor can they alter the terms of Christian communion. When addressing the sacraments, Hodge stated that valid sacraments have three parts: doing what Christ has instructed, it being carried out by a church or its authority and 'being done with the serious intention of obeying the command of Christ'. The implications of Hodge's words were transparent: Protestant refusal to recognize the legitimacy of other denomination's sacraments was erroneous. Some of the denominations, especially Baptists, dissented from these principles, but Hodge later responded graciously in writing to their criticism addressing them as his brethren that 'no difference between Baptists and Pedo-baptists can sunder'.

It was during this period that Hodge's brother died. Hugh had retired as professor of obstetrics at the University of Pennsylvania in 1864. During his years as professor, Dr Hugh Hodge published several articles for medical journals and a major book on obstetrics. He was married to Margaret Aspin

# Legacy

for thirty-eight years. The couple had seven sons, several of whom became ministers. Hugh and his family worshiped at Second Presbyterian in Philadelphia, the old Hodge family church for several generations. Hugh's wife Margaret died in 1866. In his later years Hugh suffered from blindness but kept serving on committees at Second Presbyterian Church until his death. Dr Hugh Lenox Hodge died at the end of February 1873. Charles Hodge, though ill at the time, was able to attend his brother's funeral in Philadelphia.

Charles Hodge's brother and father had been physicians, influencing his own interest in science throughout his lifetime. It was fitting that the last book Charles Hodge would write dealt with the intersection of the Bible and science. Hodge held unambiguous views on the relationship of science and Christianity. In 1859, Hodge had stated, 'God in nature can never contradict God in the Bible.' It was his conviction that all authenticated scientific 'facts' would be in full accord with the accurate interpretation of Scripture. In his *Systematic Theology*, Hodge explained how science had historically aided in the correct interpretation of Holy Scripture. He illustrated this by pointing to the medieval church's understanding of biblical cosmology according to the Ptolemaic system (earth at center of the universe). However, with conclusive evidence for the Copernican system (sun at the center), the church now universally understood creation according to the latter view. In a similar way, if geology could ultimately prove a very old earth, then this must be understood as consistent with what the Genesis account teaches. In other words, science may be an aid to interpreting Scripture, because 'Nature is as truly a revelation of God as the Bible.' Hodge interpreted the six days of Genesis as six eras of uncertain duration in which God performed his works of creation.

Alongside this balanced approach to science and the Bible, Hodge had reservations about certain theories of human origins which he believed clearly clashed with the Bible. He wrote several articles opposing ideas about different human races having diverse origins (polygenism) because this conflicted with the biblical account of all human beings descending from Adam and Eve. Biblical teachings were more certain than scientific theories. In the early 1860s, Hodge had made reference to Darwin's *Origin of Species* (1859), but not until he wrote the *Systematic Theology* did he begin significant engagement with Darwin's natural selection hypothesis. When he did finally address it, he pronounced the absence of proof for the 'mere hypothesis'. For Hodge, design in creation was fundamental to a Christian understanding of God's providence and could not be squared with random natural selection.

Eventually, Hodge would produce an entire book specifically responding to evolutionary theory: *What is Darwinism?* (1874). Darwin's second book, *The Descent of Man* (1871), was now in print, and he felt compelled to respond more fully. *What is Darwinism?* made plain that the primary objection to evolutionary theory was its denial of intelligent design behind the natural order humans observed. Denial of divine design in creation was in essence 'atheism' according to Charles Hodge. Unintelligent natural selection implied that there was no final cause, thus by implication, God did not exist. Darwin himself may have claimed to believe in God, but his theory was 'virtually the denial of God'.

# Legacy

Hodge's response to evolution was both open-minded and cautious: open to the insights of science and willing to grapple with current scientific ideas, yet always faithful to the authority of Scripture as being true in all that it teaches. Some of his fellow Presbyterian clergymen, in his day and beyond, were more embracing of Darwin's theory, asserting that evolution could be understood as God's method of creation and not necessarily a denial of God's existence. Nevertheless, Hodge clearly saw the embedded seeds of atheism at the theory's core. Especially for Calvinists, for whom the sovereignty of God was understood as central to his very being, any notion that God did not providentially govern his creation daily was outright denial of the God revealed in Scripture.

In May 1873, the Presbyterian General Assembly paid a special tribute to Hodge by visiting him in Washington. When the Assembly had gathered in Baltimore, a large portion of the body expressed a desire to see Dr Hodge, especially a number of former New School men who had never met the famed professor. Hodge was in Washington visiting relatives when the request came for him to visit the Assembly in Baltimore, which he declined due to his health. Not to be deterred, the decision was made for the Assembly to travel to Washington and greet the aged professor. Arrangements were made, and the majority of the Assembly gathered in the grand ballroom in Willard's Hotel. As Hodge entered the room, an eyewitness described him as 'very feeble and showing signs of great emotion'. The ministers gathered about him expressing their gratitude, which deeply moved him.

Reflecting on all that he had witnessed in his fifty years at the seminary, Hodge's thoughts turned to his deceased colleagues, Drs Archibald Alexander and Samuel Miller, who had laid a firm foundation for his own labors. At his fifty-year 'jubilee' celebration, when all eyes were on Hodge, he had praised the two pillars of the seminary that had made Princeton 'what it is'. In September 1874, when the seminary chapel re-opened after significant repairs, Hodge preached to the seminary community and spoke about the first two professors. The key element in their piety, said Hodge, was its Christ-centeredness. He said, 'Christ was as prominent in their religious experience, in their preaching, and in their writings, as he is in the Bible ... When students entered this Seminary, when its first professors were alive, they had held up before them the image of Christ ... It is, in large measure to this constant holding up of Christ, in the glory of his person and the all-sufficiency of his work, that the hallowed influence of the fathers of this Seminary is to be attributed.' Dr Samuel Miller Jr received a copy of the historical sermon and wrote to Hodge thanking him for the kind words spoken about his father. Samuel Miller's son added, 'I never heard him mention your name, which of course was a most familiar household word with us, excepting in terms of respect and affection.'

As admiration was heaped upon him as the prominent living Princeton professor, Hodge was mindful of being but a lowly instrument in God's hand. He was not the least bit impressed with his own contributions to the church and seminary. Near the end of his life, speaking to a friend who was praising him for his accomplishments, he replied, 'What I have done is as nothing compared with what is done by a man who goes to Africa, and labors among a heathen tribe, and reduces their language to writing. I am not worthy to stoop down and unloose the shoes of such a man.'

A blessing of Hodge's final years was having his eldest son join him on the Princeton faculty. In 1877, Archibald Alexander Hodge (1823–1886) was elected as Associate Professor of Didactic Theology at Princeton Seminary. A. A. Hodge accepted the call to assist his eighty-year-old father when the elder Hodge requested to be relieved of his teaching responsibilities. Having most recently been the professor of systematic theology at Western Theological Seminary in Allegheny, Pennsylvania, since 1864, the son now moved his family back to his hometown. Charles Hodge did not pressure him into this position but encouraged his oldest son to search his inner conscience about the matter and commit his way to the Lord.

The younger Hodge had graduated in 1846 from Princeton Seminary, where as a student he had listened to his father's lectures on theology. After graduation, A. A. Hodge and his family moved to Allahabad, India, serving as Presbyterian missionaries for three years before being forced to return because of health issues. Back in the United States, he was pastor of several congregations in Maryland, Virginia and Pennsylvania, preaching theological sermons to his congregation on Sunday evenings. In 1878, A. A. Hodge published his first book, *Outlines of Theology*, which was based upon these evening expositions on doctrinal topics and included significant material from class notes while listening to his father's lectures at Princeton. Following his labors in the pastorate, A. A. Hodge accepted the professorship at Western Seminary (renamed Pittsburgh Theological Seminary in 1959), where he taught for thirteen years.

When A. A. Hodge officially joined his father on the Princeton faculty in November of 1877, the elderly Hodge must certainly have been proud of his professor son. At his inauguration the younger Hodge delivered the lecture, 'Dogmatic Christianity, the Essential Ground of Practical Christianity'. The key point of the address was that faith and morals are inseparable, contrary to the contemporary tendency to separate the two. Truth was in order to holiness, and over-zealousness in fine points of doctrine has led to unnecessary division among Christians over unessential points. To the audience it was the clear that the son shared the spirit of his father.

The torch of teaching theology at Princeton was now passed to Archibald Alexander Hodge, only the third professor to hold this position since the seminary's founding in 1812. Fifty-four-year-old A. A. Hodge sensed the weight upon his shoulders of succeeding his father, who had followed the man for whom he was named at birth. At the conclusion of his inaugural address, he asked the board of directors to pray for him, declaring, 'Woe is me, that such a one as I should be called to inherit the responsibilities descending in such a line! ... But God has done it. He has chosen a vessel, earthen indeed, that the excellency of the power may be the more conspicuously shown forth to be His alone.'

During the final year of his life, Charles Hodge was visited by a seminary student who asked the aged professor for a motto. Hodge's reply was 'Thy Word is Truth.' The rightful place of Scripture in the life of a believer, the church, and the seminary was a major legacy of Hodge's vocation as a teacher. This mantle would be picked up by his son, Archibald Alexander, who would write one of his signature pieces just three years later, an article titled, 'Inspiration', co-authored with B. B. Warfield in 1881. B. B. Warfield (1851–1921) would become Princeton's fourth theology professor when A. A. Hodge died prematurely in 1886. Warfield would keep the Princeton heritage alive, writing numerous essays defending biblical authority, which were later collected in the volume, *The Inspiration and Authority of the Bible* (1948).

Charles Hodge spent his last years enjoying his extended family. The grandchildren who lived in Princeton visited him regularly in the study, much to his delight. He was the last survivor of the Philadelphia Hodge family, and many of his old classmates were gone. Frequently he would receive news of the death of another friend or the spouse of a friend, taking time to write a note of encouragement. The frequent visits of former students, colleagues, and friends brought him great joy. Long gone were the controversies; all that remained were his relationships with people. After a group of students visited Hodge at Princeton, one of them wrote, 'The face of our dear old professor Hodge broke out constantly into smiles of holy joy, as he sat like a father in the midst of his sons.'

In the spring of 1878, Hodge taught his classes as his strength rapidly diminished. His final Sabbath Afternoon Conference was on 14 April; the topic was 'Fight the Good Fight of Faith'. A week later he participated in the Lord's

Supper with students and faculty in the seminary chapel. As he grew weaker, he spent his days in his old chair in the study, where he had instructed students during his bout with lameness many years ago. Finally he was bedridden two days before he died. At 6.00 p.m. on Wednesday 9 June 1878, Charles Hodge was absent from the body but present with the Lord. On 22 June a funeral procession formed on the seminary grounds and made its way to First Presbyterian Church. Numerous professors and preachers participated in the service. Afterwards, his body was laid to rest in the Princeton cemetery next to his first wife Sarah. Mary Hunter Hodge would survive her husband by less than two years.

Resolutions of reverence and love, as well as editorial notices of his death, appeared in the papers of many evangelical denominations. In the *National Repository*, a Methodist magazine, the editor wrote, 'He was not only *par excellence* the Calvinistic theologian of America, but the Nestor of all American theology, and though we differ widely with him in many things, we yet accept this master mind and beautifully adorned life as the grandest result of our Christian intellectual development ... Princeton has lost its greatest ornament, the Presbyterian Church its most precious gem, the American Church her greatest earth-born luminary.' A former student observed, 'When due allowance is made for his intellect and his learning ... his chief power was in his goodness. Christ enshrined in his heart was the center of his theology and life. The world shall write upon his monument "great"; but we, his students, will write upon it "good".'

# 8

# THE IMPACT OF CHARLES HODGE'S LIFE

Contemporary scholars and students still pore over Charles Hodge's writings to explore insights into nineteenth-century American Christian experience. Due to the volume of his published work and influence on the church of his day, one cannot study this period without engaging the theological perspectives of Charles Hodge. From his professorial chair at Princeton Seminary and his public pulpit in the *Biblical Repertory*, the views of Charles Hodge helped shape Christian opinion throughout the Protestant churches of America.

To mainline Protestants, Hodge is often considered an obscurantist with unsophisticated views of Scripture, evolution, and slavery which are unacceptable to modern-thinking persons. To traditional evangelicals, he is a prince of American Calvinism, a tough-minded defender of historic Christianity against the early waves of Protestant liberalism. Historically speaking, Hodge breathed the same nineteenth-century air as everyone else of his era; however, he possessed an exceptional ability to dissect theological questions, unveiling essential issues for Christian faith. Hodge remains widely respected by those who believe in the plenary inspiration of the Bible.

No one questions the keen intellect that Hodge possessed; the story of his personal impact on those who knew him is just as impressive. His family, friends, and students testified how his life touched them in substantial ways. The professor's public life exhibited the same genuine character that his family personally experienced at home. The piety he urged upon his ministerial students was a lived reality which students sought to emulate.

A key element in his piety was the gracious spirit that pervaded all of his writings. It was said that the next best thing to being his friend was being his adversary, because he diligently tried, though imperfectly, to critique others with fairness. In modern times, when the genteel art of public debate has often been replaced with partisan meanness, Hodge's generous attitude towards opponents, political or theological, is a beacon of light. From his perspective, this was a Christian's duty.

Hodge's high view of Scripture is legendary, but he also turned to church history as a bulwark against a diluted Christianity. He would appeal to Scripture against tradition when addressing Roman Catholics and Episcopalians. But against other Protestants, including his own Presbyterian brethren, he would frequently appeal to the consensus of the faithful, though sometimes overstating the case. Christian history was valuable to Hodge, who viewed himself as an 'Augustinian', convinced that his theology was embedded in ancient Christianity as well as the sixteenth-century Protestant Reformation. In the twenty-first century, as traditional Christianity endures fierce attack, evangelicals would do well to follow Hodge's pattern, employing both Scripture and church history to defend the faith once for all delivered to the saints.

Finally, the life of Charles Hodge displayed a zeal for Christian unity. When his own Presbyterian denomination decided to re-baptize Roman Catholics, Hodge would have none of it, and chastised his brethren for denying the catholicity of the church. Addressing a gathering of Protestants from many denominations, he appealed for mutual recognition of one another's sacraments. On both counts, he encountered stiff opposition, but was undeterred in calling believers to publicly treat one another as mutual followers of Christ. Hodge's exhortations are prophetic for a divided Christendom, if Christ's people will have ears to hear.

# Recommended reading

Calhoun, David B. *Princeton Seminary*. 2 Vols. Edinburgh: The Banner of Truth Trust, 1994.

Fortson, S. Donald. *The Presbyterian Creed: A Confessional Tradition in America, 1729-1870*. Reprint, Eugene, OR: Wipf & Stock, 2009.

Hodge, Archibald Alexander. *The Life of Charles Hodge: Professor in the Theological Seminary, Princeton, NJ*. New York: Charles Scribner's Sons, 1880.

Hodge, Charles. *The Constitutional History of the Presbyterian Church in the United States of America*, Part I, II. Reprint, Philadelphia: Presbyterian Board of Publication, 1851.

*Systematic Theology*. 3 Vols. Reprint, Grand Rapids: Wm B. Eerdmans Publishing Company, 1979.

*Commentary on the Epistle to the Romans*. Reprint, Grand Rapids: Wm B. Eerdmans Publishing, 1976.

*Discussions in Church Polity*. Editor, William Durant. New York: Charles Scribner's Sons, 1879.

Hoffecker, W. Andrew. *Piety and the Princeton Theologians.* Phillipsburg, NJ: Presbyterian and Reformed Publishing Co., 1981.

*Charles Hodge: The Pride of Princeton*. Phillipsburg, NJ: Presbyterian and Reformed Publishing Co., 2011.

Noll, Mark A., editor. *Charles Hodge: The Way of Life.* Mahwah, NJ: Paulist Press, 1987.

*The Princeton Theology 1812-1921: Scripture, Science, and the Theological Method from Archibald Alexander to Benjamin Warfield*. Phillipsburg, NJ: Presbyterian and Reformed, 1983.

and David N. Livingstone, editors. *What is Darwinism? And Other Writings on Science & Religion* by Charles Hodge. Grand Rapids: Baker Books, 1994.

Stewart, John W. and James H. Moorhead, editors. *Charles Hodge Revisited: A Critical Appraisal of His Life and Work*. Grand Rapids: William B. Eerdmans Publishing, 2002.